YOU'RE THAT BITCH

& Other Cute Lessons About Being Unapologetically Yourself

BRETMAN ROCK

HarperCollins*Publishers*

**This book contains content that may not
be suitable for readers under 18.**

HarperCollins*Publishers*
1 London Bridge Street
London SE1 9GF

www.harpercollins.co.uk

HarperCollins*Publishers*
Macken House, 39/40 Mayor Street Upper
Dublin 1, D01 C9W8, Ireland

First published by HarperCollins*Publishers* 2023

1 3 5 7 9 10 8 6 4 2

Text and photographs © Bretman Rock 2023
Plant illustrations © ooddysmile/Adobe Stock
Design by Kyle O'Brien

Bretman Rock asserts the moral right to be
identified as the author of this work

A catalogue record of this book is
available from the British Library

HB ISBN 978-0-00-851148-7
TPB ISBN 978-0-00-851149-4

Printed and bound in the UK using 100% renewable
electricity at CPI Group (UK) Ltd

This book is produced from independently certified FSC™ paper
o ensure responsible forest management.

For more information visit: www.harpercollins.co.uk/green

I dedicate this entire book to my younger self, Bretman Pebble—bitch, I cry every time I think of you, and I just want you to know that your older self looks up to you so much. You are so confident and so strong, and stop worrying about the gap in your teeth—don't worry, you'll meet some really nice people who will fix it for free (you just have to post about it #ad).

CONTENTS

A Cute Intro

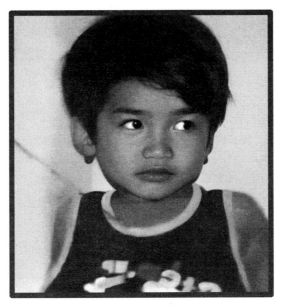

Me, age three, looking to the left because
these bitches ain't never right

Growing up in the Philippines, I loved watching my grandma Lilang get ready for church. I'd lie on her fainting couch, mesmerized by her creative choices, like which of her three lipsticks she'd choose (usually auburn) and how she'd style her kinky hair with bangs. One magical morning before church, when I was four, she came over to me and put the tiniest amount of red blush on my cheeks. It was the very first time makeup ever touched my skin. I literally went to church feeling like a girl. It was the first time I fell in love with vanity. It was the first time I ever felt like *that bitch*.

Without even realizing it, my grandma had given me my superpowers.

Since that herstorical day, I've immigrated to Hawaii from the Philippines, become a digital superstar, and have figured out how to just be unapologetically me. My impulsive, spontaneous posts—taken while beating my face, donning corsets and pearls, working out, unboxing, eating breakfast cereal, jumping off my roof, whatevah the day may bring—are watched by millions globally and have led to some of my wildest dreams coming true. Like creating a makeup line with Wet n Wild that sold out in minutes. Or sitting front row at Fashion Week, and making award-winning shows. I've been a model for Nike and a cover girl for *Playboy*. I've done commercials with Lizzo. SZA and Ariana Grande follow me on social media. I got to meet RiRi. Thinking about all these accomplishments could make me cry—I won't, though, because crying just makes me look so damn ugly.

Are you thinking, Who does this bitch think he is . . . Beyoncé? Girl, I may be writing this book at only twenty-three, but I've got stories to tell. For the last eight years I've shared so much of myself on Instagram, TikTok, and YouTube. But on social media I'm a curated brand—I don't have time to show off my full self, or to explain who I really am in addition to the jokes and glamour. So you probably know Bretman Rock the comedian and extrovert who pole dances and calls everybody "bitch," but you don't really don't know Bretman Sacayanan. These Bretmans are two different people, but they are both 1,000 percent me. And we've both lived lifetimes already. The essays you're about to read are totally fresh, sort of like goosebumps but even more tingly—they're

Me visiting me at Ulta

about being a queer first-generation Asian immigrant, who just happens to be Da Baddest content creator of all time.

I'm gonna talk more in depth about growing up in the Philippines, all of the Filipino cultural traditions and superstitions ingrained in me from an early age, being left behind with my dad when my mom and siblings moved to Hawaii, and how I learned how to speak English and become an entertainer by watching reality shows like *A Shot at Love with Tila Tequila* and *America's Next Top Model.* And obviously, a big part of who I am is about being genderqueer (I mean, did you see my *Playboy* cover?). I have lots to say about it, and I hope it will not only help other LGBTQ+ people but also open the hearts, minds, and eyes of my straight fans. Let's make one thing clear right off the bat: I identify as a human-fucking-being. I've always been a divine blend of masculine and feminine—so if I look like a lesbian after a bicep-bulging workout, call me he, but if I'm in full makeup wearing a Catholic schoolgirl plaid skirt and barrettes, call me she. I don't mind, I'm cute either way! (Maybe I should just make my own gender at this point . . . I am a Bretman.)

I'm very proud of being LGBTQ+ and Filipino, so it's an honor to be a pretty face for both underrepresented communities. Plus, Asian Americans and Asian immigrants are increasingly facing hate and violence, so I'm passionate about helping create more positive visibility for us—especially for brown Asians—in entertainment, beauty, and fashion. I want to make all of my communities proud—native, immigrant, Filipino, Hawaii.

People often ask me what my beliefs are, and the answer is simple: I believe in myself, duh! I mean, I also believe in family, and my heritage. Like I may curse like a motherfuxin' bitch, but I also embody the Aloha spirit, which is carefree, kind, spiritual, and peaceful. Back to myself: I went from living in a house with twenty-five people to owning my own home on the island of Oahu. I am the American Dream and I made it happen by hustling my whole life. I've been an entrepreneur since I was a toddler, and all of the little businesses I started as a kid—from selling feather earrings plucked straight off my cousin's cockfighting chickens to using makeup to cover up all the girls' hickeys in high school—led to my success and prepared me for this wild-ass life I created.

And what's a celebrity memoir without spilling some iced matcha latte about dating—I'll tell you about how I lost my virginity at Disneyland, about being scared of white penises, and about falling in and out of love for the first time, stuff I've never talked about publicly. [Programming note: 99.9 percent of the stories I tell are true but some names have been changed to protect those bitches.] Like, how one of my biggest accomplishments and blessings in life was not fucking anyone from my high school—I didn't date anyone the entire four years. Do not shed tears of pity for me (even if you're a cute crier)! While my classmates were busy getting STDs, I was busy becoming Bretman Rock.

You're That Bitch reflects all sides of me: I am Bretman Rock, the entertainer and an extrovert, but sometimes I also just wanna be Bretman Sacayanan in my crop top and shorts, eating my chicken unbothered. I'm just an ordinary gorl—at the same time, I'm also that bitch every minute, meaning I'm always authentically me. Sometimes I'm lazy, I get bored, I get scared, I feel ignored, I feel happy, I get silly, I choke on my own words. I've literally been diagnosed with ADHD, so like my videos and my mind, my book is organized chaos, visually gorgeous (of courz), and packed with essays, anecdotes, journal entries, and advice from my life that I want to pass on to you. Give me any topic, and I'll tell you a funny story in the way only I can. But bitch, my stories also have depth.

The full Bretman is not only what the internet sees—there are so many different sides to me. Like how I'm smarter than people think. I love learning new things and trying everything at least once. Most of all, I don't like labels, and I refuse to be pigeonholed. At the end of the day, I'm thankful for every day and every chance I get to share my light with the world—whichever facet of Bretman might be shining brightest at any given moment. So even if you're not also a genderqueer Asian influencer, I think you'll relate to my stories. These essays are about not fitting in but learning how to not give a fux, how to exude effortless confidence and win people over with charm and humor, being authentic and original, and turning your fantasies into reality the Bretman Rock way—that is, doing the least while looking the most. I want you to learn how to stop and smell the flowers and just realize: Wow, I'm that bitch, too.

Okay, I'm gonna go write about Jollibee in my journal, and get sweaty, stoned, and emotional. I hope you enjoy *You're That Bitch*. And if you don't, you can always eat a dick. I'm just kidding. I hope you have a cute day!

ONE

Born to Be Beautiful

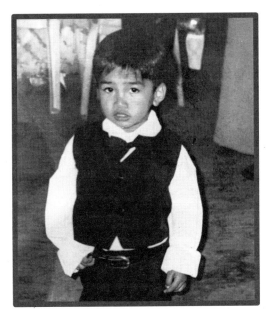

*Giving you ring bearer fantasy at
my aunt's wedding at age two*

From brown earth I was born, from fertile ground I blossom. Being beautiful is not something that describes me, it's who I *am*. It's not a hobby or a phase. I was born to be beautiful. Now, I didn't say I was *born beautiful*. Newborn babies

1

look like uncut dicks. And, damn, I was ugly as shit as a kid, but that was the past, and I'm willing to get over it. I'm actually glad I experienced being ugly, because now I know how not to look like that ever again. Being gorgeous has always been my destiny—it just took a minute.

From the minute I burst out into the world, I've rejected every binary and expectation of who I was supposed to be. The earliest memory I have from growing up in the Philippines is playing with a big blue truck that I'd bedazzled with glitter glue. I put my sister's Barbie behind the wheel and her suitcase packed with the cutest outfits into the trunk, then sent her off on her exotic adventures. I always played with boys' and girls' toys, I didn't discriminate. I built things with Legos, but it would be like a kitchen table for my Barbies. I had miniature toy soldiers, too, because someone had to guard and protect Barbie's house from dangerous bandits. My parents never walked in on me playing with dolls and freaked out like, "That's for girls, bitch!" Nobody around me ever made a big deal about it—that wasn't the environment I grew up in. My parents let me be me, because they saw a lot of both of themselves in little Bretman.

My sassiness definitely comes from my mom. That woman is a Scorpio, and she does not take shit from anyone. She's very much a my-way-or-the-highway kind of lady. But she's also really funny, and I inherited my charismatic side and the way I love talking to people from her. My mom also always likes to take credit for being my makeup role model, but bitch, no. When I was growing up, she couldn't care less about being girlie and barely ever wore makeup besides a little mascara.

People always ask me, "Who's the first beauty queen you've ever known?" Surprise, that would be my dad. He was such a metrosexual guy. He used yummy-smelling body spray, skincare products for days, and had long, luscious hair like a rock star. His hair was longer than my sister Princess's ever was growing up, and he feathered it like the guys in his favorite band, Journey. When I'd ask him, "Can you put my Barbie's hair up?," he could put it into a perfect ponytail.

My dad was a metrosexual, but at the same time he was also totally butch. It's funny because he always reminded me of Freddie Mercury from Queen. When I was little, everyone around me in the village seemed to be super skinny, and no one went to the gym. But my dad always found a way to exercise and was really into bodybuilding. He was huge by Filipino standards, a muscular guy like his WWF wrestler idols Bret "the Hitman" Hart and The Rock, who he named me after. My dad was the kind of guy women wanted and men wanted to be. He was known for being a babaeng lalake—a ladies' man. And a lot of the guys looked up to him because they could show up at our house, and my dad would always provide drinks. He was *that guy.*

Something else I drew from both of my parents as a kid: being a bit of a rascal. I constantly got in trouble for getting into physical fights with boys and girls (remember, I don't discriminate), and I also had undiagnosed ADHD, so I was a pain in my parents' asses. My dad just couldn't figure out how to keep me occupied all the time, especially before we went to church on Sundays. Everybody else in the family would be busy getting ready, and as the baby of the house (Princess hadn't been born yet), I wanted attention. First my dad told me to go outside and play with our birds—we raised pigeons, quail, and cockfighting chickens—but I kept breaking his valuable eggs. He was not happy but, still determined to tame me like a wild horse, tried buying me puzzles to stave off my boredom. I figured them out too fast, though—I was kind of a prodigy, like Beyoncé.

So after I finished my puzzles, there would be only one place left I was allowed to go—upstairs to my grandma Lilang's room. In the Philippines, my whole extended family lived in the same private compound, nine separate families in nine houses on a half acre of land. I was forbidden to go into any other rooms in our house because my auntie hated people barging in on her. (Bitch, I didn't want to see you naked, either.) But I loved wandering into my nana's room, which was the most fun anyway because it was so fucking weird. She was a witch doctor, and such a vibe. Nana had covered her walls with Chinese calendars, mirrors, and symbols, and her cupboards were filled with things I wasn't allowed to rummage through. Probably because it was like voodoo dolls and human hair and shit. I still don't fully know what the fuck that woman was ever actually up to. But I know she didn't believe in pills, even though our house was right next to a drugstore. If someone in the family had any ailment under the sun—headaches, burns, cuts, pussy itch—she had a paste for it. If I was sick, she made me drink nasty-ass potions; she could have peed in them, and I'd have no idea.

Nana Lilang had a signature lewk—a hunch and curly short hair with bangs. She also always wore the same dusty-rose-colored shirt with holes in it. It was her security blanket. She had a ton of other cute clothes, but she washed and wore this one raggedy-ass pink shirt every single day—she would literally be buried in it when she passed, when I was in fourth grade.

Besides the shirt, Nana took great pride in her appearance, especially when she was getting ready for church—she needed to show off for the other girls. It was a ritual, and while she beat her face sitting at her little makeup table, I'd lie on her mahogany fainting couch and pepper her with questions about the process. I was mesmerized by her creative choices. I could sit there and watch my grandma for hours, but sometimes she put me to work and had me color her hair with the cheap dye from the drugstore next door, or pay me to pluck out her white hairs. (OMG—I just realized that was my first-ever paying job, and I was just a toddler!)

Sometimes my grandma got frustrated with me. I was one of those "Why?" kids who needed everything explained to me. "Why is it called Sunday?" "Why do we go to church?" "Why are we going to burn in hell?" But she was the only person who never scolded me, and she always answered all my questions, no matter how stupid or annoying. My grandma was an angel, and I was always by that bitch's side growing up. I was like her shadow.

Remember the story that I mentioned in the intro, about the magical morning Nana Lilang put makeup on my face for the first time? Let me finish telling you the full story. When I was four, I was standing by her vanity as she got ready for church and firing off my usual barrage of whys. When I asked, "Why does blush make your face red?" she turned to me and, with the kindest smile, put the tiniest amount of red blush on my cheeks. I did a happy dance—girl, I was really feeling myself, and I'll never forget her laughter and joy watching me. That was the first time I fell in love with vanity. My grandma gave me the superpower of feeling like *that bitch.*

I felt so pretty and couldn't wait to leave the house and be out in public with my fiery cheekbones. I went to Catholic church that morning feeling like a girl. I was so fishy in my mind, like my hair was touching my asshole. Before we walked through the front door of the chapel, I cupped my hands together and dunked them in the two angel figurine bowls right next to the entrance, then drenched myself in holy water, ready to get on my knees and pray to whoever God was. It was truly a religious experience.

My grandma Lilang was the first person in my family to actively signal to me that it was okay to openly express my feminine side. I don't know what the fuck I did to her for her to love me that much, but from that moment with the blush on, I felt like it was me and her versus the world. She was also the first person in my family to tell me it was okay to be gay, too—when our priest talked about how two men sleeping together was wrong, she'd lean over and whisper to me, "Don't listen to him—he's not always right." Duh, Nana! I already wasn't paying attention at mass to begin with.

The Philippines are super Catholic, and it's not the most progressive place in the world, so it's actually pretty shocking how almost nobody ever messed with me about being gay when I was growing up. I think people could sense that my parents and grandma knew I was gay but didn't give a fuck. Also, my dad was this big muscular guy, so even if they had a problem with me being gay, they knew to keep it to themselves, bitch.

My dad was never the best husband, but he was a really great father to me, and I think it had a lot to do with my grandma Lilang, his mom, being so open first. (I'm pretty sure she told him I was gay, and he accepted me without ever actually telling me that he accepted me.) We had a local illegal lottery called Jueteng, and my dad always bet a few pesos when the people who ran it came by, using my birthday, 731. One time his number came up, and he won enough money to buy us a tricycle: basically an electric motorbike that had a sidecar. We tooled around everywhere together in that tricycle, me riding shotgun. If he skipped church, we'd ride over when it was closed, and he'd guiltily drop some coins into the donation box outside.

He also took me to work with him. My dad had a twin brother, and they owned a transportation company called . . . Twin Bros Transportation, don't @ me. I'm not gonna lie, for a long time I couldn't tell my dad and uncle apart, and it confused me. Sometimes when my dad would travel for work for a long time, I'd cry, and my uncle would pretend to be my dad so I wouldn't get upset. It was only when my uncle broke his fucking leg and got crutches that I realized which one was which and that I'd been bamboozled my entire first few years of life.

For work, my dad and uncle would drive buses to the rice paddies and farms outside of town so people could load up fruits, vegetables, and rice to bring back and sell at the local market. I sat next to him while he drove, and he made me his official conductor. If I couldn't go with him that day, he'd bring home Jollibee for dinner—two chickens with gravy and rice to cheer me up. You don't understand, where we lived, there were no big restaurants and stuff like that—it wasn't a rich village or anything—so it was very cool of him. I would literally be crying and fucking eating the bones and toes because it was such a luxury. I knew my dad loved me unconditionally, even when I ate my chicken like an animal. "Are you sure you're gay?" he'd ask me. "That's not how gay people eat."

My uncle liked to tease me, too. One time I was eating a peanut butter sandwich, wearing a cute little red and blue jersey jacket with the letter *B* on it that my mom got me.

"The B is for Bretman." I beamed.

"Are you sure it doesn't stand for 'baklâ'?" my uncle said, laughing. *Baklâ* is Filipino for "fag."

My dad picked up my sandwich and threw it at his brother. "Don't ever call him that again!" he yelled. I really wanted that fucking sandwich, but it was so sweet of my dad to do that. It was the first time anyone ever defended me for being a flaming homosexual. And you know what? My uncle never called me baklâ again.

After that, if other people made comments about me being gay, I remember my dad would shoot back, "He's gonna make me rich one day." Such a cute burn.

Insecurity was something I never really struggled with because all that early support from my family kind of made me feel unstoppable. I meet so many queer people with such different growing-up and coming-out stories, and I start thinking like, I never even had to come out, and all of that is because I had the luxury of a very open and accepting family, who made me feel seen and let me explore my gender. There is so much power in acceptance. Acceptance created the bad bitch I am today.

My grandma will never know just how powerful her implicit acceptance would become for me. In Filipino families, we often have a totem we pass down to future generations. On my mom's side of the family, it's her mom's necklace, and on my dad's side, it's a ring from my grandpa. I feel like that simple act of putting blush on me that day was my grandma passing a totem to me. Even though I probably sweated it off from running around the church five minutes after I got there, it meant the world to me. And as I grow older, I've come to see it more and more as a moment where she handed her powers over to me. When I put on makeup, I think of her. And when I look in the mirror, I see beauty everywhere, even in my uneven eyelids, because one of them looks like my grandma's eyelid, and one of them looks like my grandpa's.

Now, whenever people ask me, "When was the first time you wore makeup?" I think about my nana laughing and smiling as I peacocked in her witchy room, and it still makes my heart warm. That was the moment I realized you can do anything when you're really feeling yourself. You can do anything you want when you're a bad *bitch*.

Crystals I travel with

Finding Connection

There's a word in Filipino, kapwa, which means your connection not just with yourself but with other people. Lately I've been thinking about my grandmother and her witchy herbs, and how both sides of my family were rice farmers and worshipped water for generations—you know, you water the plants and crops so that we can eat. As I've gotten older (and even wiser, girl), I've realized that kapwa isn't just your family and friends and human communities but also your relationship with the earth and everyone on it, living and nonliving things. I think, in order to find your inner bitch, you're gonna need to be able to make these connections—to find that fierce energy within yourself, within other people and living beings around you, and channel that energy back out, in bigger and bigger circles of nurturing. You know, like you care about your family, and then you care about the environment that you're in, and ultimately all of that care, love, and acceptance kind of cycles (Get it? Like the water cycle?) back to you. Period.

TWO

Halo, Asong Babae

The biggest question that everyone has always asked me, even way before I was anyone, is: "Why are you like this?" or "What are you on?" (Which breaks my heart, because nobody ever asks, "What are you under?")

I can't help who I am. I don't think it's possible for me to be any other way than "this." I'm the definition of being a product of my environment. I mean, I was born and raised in the Philippines, a country that literally shuts down to watch the Miss Universe pageant. There are so many Filipino influences that made me the bad bitch I am today, from speaking three languages (Ilocano, Tagalog, and English) to how hard I brush my teeth.

My hometown, Sanchez-Mira in the province of Cagayan, sits on a seaside peninsula at the tippy top of the Philippines, about six hours away from the capital, Manila. I think it's like six hours? It depends on traffic and road conditions. And when I say "road," girl, that's open to interpretation. There aren't really stop signs or established lanes marked with lines, so the journey is always chaotic and unpredictable (kind of like me). When you're on the road, you kind of just pray you don't get hit.

The Philippines is a wild country. Third world (which I know isn't the phrase we use anymore, but it was while I was growing up there) did not even feel like the way to describe what it was like then—if anything, our village felt like fourth world. No, *fifth world*. Don't get it twisted, I didn't say it's not beautiful, okay? I grew up surrounded by jungle, mountains, and black sand beaches nestled on clear blue seawater. My tiny rural town—population two thousand bad bitches—is an agricultural potpourri, teeming with rice paddies and cornfields, pineapple and banana farms, and fruit trees: coconut, cacao, and coffee. We had it all—frogs and little animals were obsessed with the abundance of crops we had, and then every winter, the grey-faced buzzards (or sawi, as locals call them), would migrate there to feast their ugly little faces off on the frogs.

Whatever food the frogs and the motherfuxin' buzzards left for the rest of us would be put on buses, like the ones my dad and uncle drove, and brought back to be sold by vendors at the central market. How do I even describe the market? It was right next to the river and smelled like dead fish, goat carcass, and chicken shit. I swear to God they would murder cows straight up inside the market, it really did smell like death. I feel like I'd need to make a Google Maps to explain the layout of the market to you, but it also changed every day . . . it was so disorganized and chaotic.

One day a week the market transformed into a flea market where you could buy furniture, medicine, cleaning equipment, and school supplies, which is what my mom sold. I'd usually go and bother her at the market and take things like shoes from our own store. You could find the cheapest things there, things that you never even thought you needed, like pellet guns. Everything cost a peso, the equivalent of a nickel. My dad would give me five pesos every day—one peso got me chips and my favorite snack, a green mango pickled in a vinegar juice concoction, thicc as Bisquick, which came in a little baggie. With the leftover pesos I'd buy baby duck hatchlings that I'd bring home to add to our coops and take care of. Or if I was feeling like a generous little bitch, I'd treat my friends to a snack.

A lot of kids would be like, "You came to school with five pesos in your pocket? Girl, are you a billionaire up in this shit?"

In first grade, I'm not gonna lie, I *was* a bougie kid. My family was considered a little wealthier than most people in town. So I had a driver who took me to school in my dad's electric tricycle. And I had two babysitters who fed me and gave me sponge baths in bed when I refused to get up for school. (I guess it was more like a whore's bath—just the pits and the naughty bits.) Okay, I exaggerated, the "driver" was my cousin, and if I didn't get out of bed after like fifteen minutes, I'd get my ass beat. No need to call social services, besties—in the Philippines, all children get their asses beat. Every Filipino kid's worst nightmare is seeing a shoe, stick, belt, or slipper because you *will* get hit with it.

We weren't actually rich, just above average for where we lived, and we never went hungry because my extended family all worked in catering and owned a bunch of restaurants. On the family compound there were people everywhere and tons of animals and birds running around our property at all times. Every morning I'd wake up to the aroma of pinakbet, adobo, and sinigang cooking in giant clay pots, wafting in my bedroom window.

13

For breakfast, my auntie would serve us a dish of chicken breast and rice with banana ketchup, and girl, I gobbled that up so fast. I don't even remember what other ingredients were in it, but it gave me all the energy I needed for the rest of the day. But I never took having plentiful food for granted. I've always eaten moderately (even if I'm not eating slowly) because I was taught from the day I was born, "You eat until you're full," periodt. As soon as you're full, you stahp.

Our compound was really cool—between the nine families, we were like a modern-day tribe. I mostly hung out with my cousins, like Keiffer, aka Miss Kay. Growing up, I didn't even know they were my cousins. I didn't know what a cousin was! I just thought I had so many friends. I found out later they were all just required to be my friends cuz they were my blood relations.

Our town was made up of mostly large clans like ours. Our entire community was so tight-knit, it was almost a cult. Like, if you wandered into my town and asked anyone where my family lived, they'd be like, "Oh sure, go down to the third rice paddy, make a right at the white cow, and it's second house from the jail." There were no secrets in my hometown. If somebody killed somebody, everybody would know who did it and everybody would go to the funeral. Probably even the killer and her family, too.

I did have some neighborhood friends who I wasn't related to. Melony, who we called Ading Ading, which means "Baby Baby," was my first girlfriend. We played balay balay—the direct translation is "house house." Don't ask me why we say everything twice. Twice is nice, bitch. People always told me and Melony to kiss, and I'm ashamed to say I succumbed to peer pressure more times than I want to admit. (Please don't take away my gold-star lesbian badge.) Melony and I planned a faux wedding, something

I couldn't pretend to do with my other friends because they were my cousins, and it'd be weird if I married my cousins. We may have been in a developing country, but we weren't motherfuckin' Alabama. (JK, love you Alabama.) Even though I already knew I was gay, I remember being totally into the wedding because I loved being the center of attention. I played an excellent husband. You could say I was the greatest actress since Darna, the Philippines' most famous comic superheroine. Darna was our version of Wonder Woman. I'd watched all of Darna's shows and movies as a kid, and identified with her because she loved swallowing balls (in times of danger, she would swallow a round white stone to transform into a badass bikini-clad superhero bitch). If I wasn't watching *Darna*, I'd be watching other super girlie shows, like *Winx Club*.

Anyway, bitch, Melony and I exchanged vows, we kissed, we put a rock in her stomach, pretending it was a baby, and she gave birth to my cousin Niña. That's what we did for fun, pretended to have babies. Some people grow up with expensive video consoles like PlayStation, but our broke asses had to make up games. Another one was tumbang preso, a mash-up of lawn bowling and kick-the-can. You put a slipper on top of a can, run a hundred yards out, and throw another slipper at the can. Once the slipper is knocked off the can, you run and put it back on the can. That's at least an hour of free entertainment. We also played the pobrecita version of dodgeball. We didn't have rubber balls, so we found small rocks, covered them with crumpled paper, and threw them at each other. Don't worry, bebé, we *did* make sure the rocks were small enough not to take out an eye or cause permanent brain damage.

When you got nuthin', honey, you gotta get creative. We did

not have a playground. We didn't have a jungle gym; we had the real motherfuckin' jungle in our backyards, with legit anacondas, water snakes, scorpions, flying frogs, three-foot-tall monkey-eating eagles, and fruit bats the size of a toddler. All the parents knew if they needed to find their kid, we were probably somewhere deep in the jungle throwing extravagant weddings in our makeshift tree houses. Or collecting snails. On rainy days, if the jungle flooded, all the snails got washed down into the fields. Before they could eat all the rice, the kids would be put in charge of snatching up the snails and selling them at the market. A pound of snails earned you five pesos—enough to buy this beetch more candy and soda pops from my favorite sari-sari.

I *loved* to buy tasty snacks from street vendors with my allowance or hard-earned snail cash. Food just tastes so much better when you pay for it yourself. It's also so Asian—not just a Filipino thing—to eat a lot of street food. Every street in my town had tons of stalls. My favorites sold barbecue, balut, lumpia, fried banana fritters wrapped in wet banana leaves, silky tofu, and a refreshing creamy fruit juice called sago't gulaman, doled out of big colorful jars with ladles.

Also being business-savvy is in my blood. In addition to selling school supplies at the market once a week, my mom also sold fruit and vegetables in our designated stall on the other days, and like a good little carny and a natural-born salesman, I'd help her out, since I wasn't in school yet at that point. But my first serious job was working for my auntie. She was really into plants and would always need fertilizer, so she'd give me a bunch of bags and say, "Fill these up and I'll give you ten pesos for each bag." I literally picked up cow shit with my bare hands to earn those pesos. You might be like, Ew, you nasty boy, but I would not have traded that experience for anything—I didn't even feel like I was working because it was so fun! Listen, a little shit-stain never hurt nobody. When we were in the jungle, if we had to go number two, it's not like we could run all the way home, so we'd wipe our asses with whatever we could find, leaves, sticks, stones. Back when I was a bully for a hot minute, I'd throw poo-covered sticks at my friends. Precious memories.

My family and I were barely ever indoors, not matter how hot and humid it was. Girl, let me tell you, you don't know hot and humid until you experience the Philippines from August to October. It's rare to see anyone in jeans because the air's so muggy and heavy. I'd like to say I've been into fashion from an early age, but girl, there was just no fashion where I came from. Fashion doesn't exist in tiny village in a tropical hothouse. It's just not a priority. Nobody dressed up, there was no such thing as "fancy." We only had two seasons—wet and dry—and either way, you were gonna be soaked, whether from sweat or rain. You glistened all day, every day, and not in the zexy way. I actually don't think it's a joke that the Philippines does not have an ozone layer. The air is dirty and sticky, and the sun pushes through it to just punch you. There's a stereotype that Filipinos take multiple baths per day, but that one's true. You shower, you go outside, you play for an hour, you're dirty and sticky again, you get back in that shower. All of this also explains why I'm usually in some state of shirtless to this day.

And don't even get me started on rainy season. I lived in the north, literally the typhoon capital of the Philippines. We would get hit first, every year at the same time in October. But as scary as typhoons and flash floods and landslides are, we learned from an early age to celebrate the rain. It's going to come regardless, but you know what always comes after the rain? Rice and rainbows. Filipinos see the rain as an opportunity to not water their plants for a week. If there's one thing about Filipinos, no matter what we're going through, in general, we're going to find the silver lining. Instead of complaining, we know the skies will eventually clear up and life goes on.

Filipinos are the most optimistic, resilient people on the planet, and I love that. Like, we might have gotten colonized and forced to convert to Catholicism, but let me tell you, people like my nana Lilang were still low-key practicing our ancient spirituality, keeping altars and sneaking in our traditional icons for worship by hiding them beneath, like, a statue of Mother Mary. And still showing up with a full face beat for the Lord on Sundays. Or when my whole town was flooded, girl, we were out on our roofs doing karaoke. Filipinos love to sing, and they can belt. Unfortunately, while I got the gene for every other stereotypical Filipino thing there is, singing skipped me for some reason. Do I think I can sing? Absolutely. Does anybody else think I can sing? Absolutely not. (But whether I'm good or not, I will sing. I really do think I'm Beyoncé.)

And if you think I'm funny, bitch, everyone in the Philippines is funny—we literally cannot outfunny each other. It was only when I moved to America that I saw so many distraught people all over the place. It was so weird to me, like Wow, what's wrong with everyone? That was the exact opposite attitude to the one where I grew up. Where I come from, we're literally always looking for any reason to celebrate.

I mean, my fellow countrymen, -women, and everyone in between celebrate Christmas for six months straight. We actually call it "Bermas" because once the months turn to the Bers (September, October, November, December), you are legally allowed to go Christmas caroling. Imagine it being September and you hear people singing "Deck the Halls" outside your house. I mean, I can belt out "Ang Pasko ay Sumapit" with the best of them, and I'll even add in my own ad-libbed lyrics such as "Open the fuckin' door, bitch," but after month two even I'm like, Please stahp. And when I tell you that they will continue caroling all the way up to January, I'm not kidding. After January, we get started on Chinese New Year's. My family isn't ethnically Chinese, but we're out here celebrating Chinese New Year's.

Whatever it is, we'll celebrate it, even if it has nothing to do with us. Filipinos are very passionate people. Some might say we go a little too far. We all worship the crown—and I'm not talking about Meghan and Harry, though I do love me a little ginger spice boo. No, girl, we are obsessed with pageants. Miss Universe is our version of the Super Bowl, especially after Miss Pia Wurtzbach won in 2015, the first time the Philippines had won in almost two decades, but Steve Harvey read the wrong name, Miss Colombia, off the prompt card. The whole moment was kind of taken away from Miss Pia because they literally gave her the crown with only ten seconds left on air to do her first walk, you know, since the whole thing is still a live program. Anyways, when Miss Universe happens, everybody calls off from work and the whole country tunes in and roots for our homegrown girl to bring home the tiara. Since the 2000s, Philippines has always made top twenty of Miss Universe. I don't know why all of this fuxin' Miss Universe knowledge is coming through right now, this is literally like how straight men are so passionate when you talk to them about NFL and how many rings they've got, like, that's how

19

we are with pageants, bitch. Don't play with us. But we're just as invested in any pageant, big or small—Miss Globe, Miss Earth, Miss Moon, Miss Sky, whatever. If anyone throws on a sash that says "Miss Philippines," they will inherit 111 million rabid fans immediately, no questions asked. We just love pretty things, and we're always so excited when anyone represents the Philippines for any reason.

Pageantry is genuinely a huge part of Filipino culture. We don't just obsessively watch pageants on TV, we also throw them in every city throughout the country almost every day of the year. My family was usually very involved in our town's pageants in some way—we would sometimes be the official sponsors, some-times the caterers, and at the very least donate chairs. Our town held our pageants in our town hall or the coliseum (which was actually an old beat-up basketball court), and of course I was ob-sessed with them. We had pageants for kids, pets, people, places, and things that didn't even make sense—like, my town once held a pageant only for women who worked in the rice fields. The best ones were the gay pageants, though, which, in hindsight, was pretty revolutionary to have in a town as small as ours. These bitches . . . the talent, I was in awe. One might be dancing, one might be spitting fire, one might be singing, one might be doing a Filipino folk dance. I was like, OMG, gays are talented as fux.

Did I want to be in the pageants? Oh God, please, duh, you don't even need to ask. Sadly, I never got to, but one of my neigh-bors was a contestant and I rooted for her with all of my heart and soul and, if I remember correctly, with earsplitting high-pitched squeals. Every year I still get asked to go back to my hometown and judge that year's gay pageant. (I love that they keep asking me. One day I *will* be home right around the time. . . .)

My mom actually won a pageant once. It was for the weirdest category—"Mrs. Balikbayan," the Tagalog word for "Mrs. Coming Home." She'd started traveling to America to make more money for the family, and she'd just returned from a work trip to Hawaii. She was up against two other middle-aged women who had also gone to America and come back home. For the Mrs. Balikbayan crown, there was no swimsuit competition, no baton twirling, no Q&A asking how they'd solve climate change. Yenno what they had to do? These three women had to get lined up in three chairs in a stadium, with boxes placed in front of each. Then everybody in that stadium went up and dropped money into the box of the woman they wanted to vote for, and whoever got the most donations was the winner. My mom won, duh, because she literally put her own money in the box. She did not hold back—she handed out wads of cash to her friends so they could stuff the ballot box. Listen, I was not raised by a loser. There's a reason why I'm a sore loser today—I do not come from good sportsmanship people. My mom rigged a whole pageant so she could win. Let me tell you, she has zero shame about it, and is still so proud of her sash.

After my mom "won" her pageant, we had a parade for her. In the Philippines you only need the smallest reason for us to throw you the grandest parade—we love them just as much as we love pageants. One time word got around town that our mayor had been selected to be a contestant on the Filipino reboot of the game show *Deal or No Deal*. The idea that someone from our little city was chosen to be on television was such a huge fuckin' deal that my town threw an extravagant (even by our standards) farewell party for her. There was music and food and dancing. "Congrats, Mayor!" everyone shouted. "Bring home the million!"

21

Then we could be rich as a town, and we'd be so proud. The mayor soaked in all the attention—and conveniently forgot to mention to us any time before, during, or after the event that her upcoming appearance on *Deal or No Deal* was only a rumor. Nobody had bothered to check if the gossip was true! Girl, tell me why we had a whole party for her? The whole town was ready for her to leave. We were parading for this woman to win. And then . . . she never went. Nobody got mad at her, though. I mean, what are you going to get mad at? We all got fed, and everybody had a great time.

Having a great time is a Filipino's primary goal in life. So our barangay—the local government—always made sure we have plenty of festivals to attend. Whether we were celebrating abal-abal (June beetles, an annual delicacy that we only harvest in the fall) or suman latik (rice cakes wrapped in banana leaves and a sweet caramel sauce), festivals gave us the opportunity to socialize, drink, dance, and wear costumes made out of coconut leaves, bark, and fruit. Tell that bitch Heidi Klum we made dresses out of corn husks way before *Project Runway*. (JK, hi Heidi, love you, miss you.)

We usually strove to be joyful and happy as much as possible, except for one special day a year: Day of the Dead, on November 1. We get really serious with that shit. Especially in the provinces, like, bitch, it's a shutdown—nobody's allowed out, and you're not allowed to make any noise. From the minute you wake up to the minute you put your head back on your pillow, the streets are empty and everybody's praying at home. There are no kids running around and no tricycles zigzagging down the street. It's the opposite of how Halloween is celebrated in the United States—everyone in America goes out trick-or-treating, and it's not even a celebration of the dead. It's just an excuse for some people to dress up like a ho. Which I'm not mad about. Some years I dress up like a ho, too. Other years I throw on a black wig, black glasses, and a long black leather trench coat to transform into the fahbulous Edna Mode from *The Incredibles.*

On Day of the Dead back home, every house has an altar, whether somebody's dead in your immediate family or not. Some altars get really cute. You lay out a cross or a statue figure, Mother Mary or Jesus. You fill up a bowl with sticky rice, but you don't cook the sticky rice. Then you put an egg on it, but you don't cook the egg either because apparently it gets cooked in heaven. You pray over it, but you don't eat it because it's for the dead. Then you just sit in your house quietly, which was almost impossible for me as a kid. But somehow I managed, because I respect the dead, bitch. And I respect our traditions. The phrase I always heard growing up, especially when I heard my Tagalog friends getting scolded by their parents, was, "Aren't you ashamed of what others will think?" Whether our parents know it or not, they taught us respect and humility really, really young.

We might live for the glamour of a celebration, but everything about Filipino culture is also designed to keep people humble. Especially the folklore. Adults used it expertly to keep us kids out of trouble. Like, if we were rowdy, or stayed out too late in the forest, or frolicked on the beach during high tide, our parents and grandmas reminded us about all the aswangs, shapeshifting mythical creatures that would get us if we weren't good.

There was Manananggal, the aswang who severed her own torso, turned into a bat, and would suck your blood out.

Tiyanak, who disguised itself as a baby, and would eat whoever picked it up when it cried.

And the dreaded Tiktik, whose long black tongue slithered

23

down chimneys, then ripped out and ate the fetuses from pregnant women's stomachs. Damn, girl, there was lots of baby-eating in Filipino folklore . . . whatever it took to scare us straight. (But don't worry, I would never be actually straight, no matter what supernatural ghoul was trying to kill me.)

Filipino folklore has been passed down from so many generations, but adults would also pull random shit out of their asses to get us to obey them. Let's say I wouldn't eat my dinner. My mom would shame me with: "You have to eat every piece of rice on your plate, because you know what happens to the rice if you don't eat it? It goes back into the jungle, crying. Is that what you want to see?"

If I got in a fight with my sister, my mom would say, "Bretman, you know what happens when you fight girls, right?"

"What?"

"You're going to start growing boobs."

Then I'd beat my sister up even more. Don't threaten me with a good time, bitch.

I have reasons to believe that Filipino grandmas were the ones who invented the word *superstition* because I swear, they are experts at making shit up on the spot. I could be playing basketball at night and then my grandma would warn, all dramatic, "Bretman, you know what happens when you bounce balls at night?"

"What, Grandma?"

"The centipedes fall from the sky."

Bitch, I would believe her.

"There's no cutting nails on the weekends," she might say out of the blue one day.

"Why don't you cut your nails on the weekends, Grandma?"

24

"Because it's bad luck, and no money will come to you."
Who says that? I'll tell you. Every old Filipino woman. These
ladies of all ages have got superstitions for days, especially when
they're pregnant. Don't get mad at your husband too much when
you're pregnant, because the baby will end up looking like him.
My cousin's mom wanted her baby to be pretty, so she rubbed her
belly while looking at a Barbie doll, and boom, her daughter really
did turn out looking like a Filipino Barbie doll when she grew up.
If that sounds crazy, I'm not done, bitch. The biggest superstition
is that whatever craving a pregnant woman has will affect what
form their kid will take. My mom craved balut eggs while she was
pregnant with me (I also love them now), and my whole family
thinks I'm hairy because when the ducks are in the egg, they still
have hair. I *am* the only one in my family besides my grandpa who
can grow a beard. (Well, I used to be able to before I lasered my
gorilla mask off. Sadly, you can still see little stubbles because the
laser didn't get everything. Not cute.)

I could go on and on, name all of my family members, and tell
you what their moms' craving were when they were pregnant. But
that would take forever. Okay, fine, I'll just do a few of my favorites: My auntie had cravings for crabs, and my cousin was born
with two fingers on each hand. My cousin's mom had cravings for
adobo dog, a delicacy back home, and now my cousin laughs like
a dog and pants when he's tired. With my niece Cleo, my sister
had cravings for laing, a popular dish made with dried taro leaves
and coconut milk. The first couple of months of Cleo's life, we
thought something was wrong with her because her shit looked
like laing (for all the Americans reading this, picture spinach dip
that sat out in the sun all day). My mom was like, "See, that's why
I told you not to eat laing." Mothers know best, bitch. Then I have

another auntie who craved squid, and her son came out really dark, the darkest one in the family. Of course, you know, there's no problem with that. But sadly, a lot of Filipinos believe you have to eat a lot of mangoes when you're pregnant so that your baby will come out whiter.

America has a spectrum of racism, but the Philippines primarily has a specific version of it, what we call "colorism"; an internalized bias that favors lighter skin, which has been a thing pretty much ever since the Spanish explorer Magellan colonized our country in the 1500s. Where I'm from, in the north, is where a lot of native Filipinos like me and my family live—we are typically Moreno, meaning browner or darker-skinned, with flatter noses and curly hair. I hated my curls growing up, so I would always straighten them to the point that I ruined the curl pattern on the ends of my hair. Being Moreno is considered not beautiful under colorism, while being light-skinned or Mestizo (mixed) and straight-haired is idealized and idolized. Almost all of our celebrities and pageant queens are Mestizo or maputi (light-skinned).

It's very common for stars and regular people alike to bleach their skin. Fuck common, it's more like an epidemic. My country has one of the highest rates of use of skin lighteners in Asia. If you went to the Philippines today, you'd see billboards everywhere for soaps, mercury-laced creams, pills, and injection treatments that claim to whiten skin. The ads show before pics of sad tan girls and after pics of happy whiter girls. The message screams, "If you're white, you're beautiful." You see that everywhere you go. Store shelves are packed with products made with glutathione, a lightening ingredient that's not even approved for use in the States. But Filipinos all strive for that light skin anyway. Even yours truly did at one point, which might make you look at my

26

current perfect, caramel-colored body and cry, "Why, Bretman, whyyyyyyyy?"

When I was young, I wanted to be Mestiza so badly, I asked my mom to bring me home papaya soap, one of the natural ingredients that allegedly lightens skin. I hated being Moreno; it was a word I refused to identify with for years, until after we moved to America. I brainwashed myself into thinking I was a Mestiza girl, though obviously I wasn't. It was something I really struggled with, growing up. That type of self-hatred shit is so toxic.

It wasn't until very recently that I embraced my Moreno skin shade. I honestly didn't realize I was experiencing the effects of colorism until I moved to Hawaii, which, girl, is the closest state to the equator, where the sun shines 270 days a year. I was gonna get darker after moving—I didn't have a choice. But the first time I went home after I got sort of famous, sitting in studios and meetings with Filipino celebrities, I couldn't help but compare my skin tone to them. Our mainstream media is not brown. People who book jobs are not native Filipino. When you watch Filipino films, the workers are darker, and the rich ones are lighter. That's the sad part. A role could call for an Indigenous Aeta woman and they would hire a half-white, half-Filipino woman and paint her skin black just so she can play a maid. Blackface is still a thing on our TV shows, and it's just not discussed back home. That's the ignorance that I grew up in, and brought with me when I first came to America.

The Filipino version of racism is really not that much different than anywhere else in the world. The only difference is, in the States, we are more woke about our racism—we mostly know it's a problem. What sets the Philippines, and most other Asian countries, apart is that we still don't see colorism as a problem. It's not that nobody calls it out, it's just hard to call out when a lot of Filipinos continue to lighten their skin. If I think really hard about it, I personally can't think of or name anyone as tan as me who's famous back home. That's why when I shot my first magazine cover for *Nylon*, I gave a shout-out to all my dark-skinned Filipino brothers and sisters. To see any brown person on a famous fashion mag cover meant so much to so many people, including me, bitch. It was a magical moment, like, "Look Mom, I'm a fucking cover girl!" I wrote on my Instagram captions, "This is for all the baklâs" and "Proud to be Moreno."

Just a few years ago, it would have been unthinkable for me to write that. Today, I'm embracing what it means to be a true Filipino, and every part of my upbringing, history, and heritage has made me the Bretman I am today—a happy, humble, dark-skinned ingenue.

Next time I go back, I think I want a parade for the Morenos and the baklâs.

Aunties, make me a sash and set up the chairs!

Celebrate Your Culture but Also Question It

I think a lot of immigrants and second-generation kids can go too far in the other direction when we try to assimilate into a new country. Like, right now I'm trying to decolonize my spiritual practice and work in some of the rituals my grandmas used to do, and do less westerny stuff. I stopped following the zodiac and smudging my house with sage, as much as I loved it, and I'm trying to study more native Filipino stuff and what we believed instead. I think it's v. important to stay connected to your roots, but at the same time stay open to the idea that maybe some of the old country ways and ideas and traditions can be super flawed, too.

Something I had to process was the Filipino obsession with whiteness. I hear often about how Asian Americans don't see themselves on Western TV and stuff like that. I also didn't see myself a lot when I moved to America, but I think it'll shock a lot of people when I say that even in Filipino showbiz, Filipino media, I don't see myself on TV back home. Back home whiteness is glamorized— being light means power. If you're wealthier, it means you can stay out of the sun. You're not working in the fields.

When I went back home that time for Miss Universe, I saw the biggest faces and stars endorsing lightening products. The thing is, because they're using chemicals to look white, I noticed that their skin almost looks dead. It's not a healthy white glow. And yet, being back in the Philippines, looking at all of them, I still wanted that too. I'm ashamed to admit it wasn't that long ago that I felt so insecure about my own skin color that I went to a world-renowned Filipino aesthetician and walked out of there with five soaps and lotions, one face-lightening cream, and another cream for my taint because I was like, Dammmn doctor, even my hole's dark.

But when I got back to Hawaii, I said to myself, What are you doing, bitch? As I read more about our history, I've realized that these racist biases were brought over by our white Spanish coloniz-ers. When we're told that beauty means white, we're like okay, fine, we'll be white. I had a major epiphany then: we want to be our own oppressor. By the time I went home again, a couple of years after the Miss Universe gig for work, it was comedic to me how badly people wanted to be white. Y'all don't even understand how blessed you are to have skin that doesn't burn when you go out in the sun. You get darker, cuz that's just how much your skin loves you. Be glad you turn brown and not red. What I'm trying to say is, learn your history, honor your traditions, but also keep your eyes and ears open for what maybe needs a little updating and zhuzhing up. And appreciate your uniqueness. We all don't need to look like the same brand of white—we have to have diversity in this world, even if the media doesn't celebrate it.

THREE

Bitches Be Fighting for Me

W hen you're three years old, you don't really give a fux about anything other than your toys. So when my mom and my two siblings packed up and moved to Hawaii without me, leaving me behind with my dad, to be honest I was way more preoccupied with the guilt gift she bought me—a new ride-on truck stuffed with Barbie dolls—than heartbroken. Back then, in the Philippines, that kind of toy was not common. I was like, Girl, is this the future? What's next, flying cars?

We dumped 80 percent of my family off at the airport, and I was all "Girl, bye," without a care in the world. Well, actually, I had one major concern—the Barbies my mom left in the truck turned out to be all the meth-addicted-looking bitches my little sister didn't want anymore—she took all the pretty ones with her. And they needed head-to-toe makeovers STAT. Regardless, I was still very happy with my haul.

I don't fux with skanky hos because they are a bad reflection on me, so I made my new Barbies beautiful dresses out of tissue paper, leaves I found outside, and scraps from my grandma's curtains and tablecloths. Grandma Lilang even helped me sew them together because she was an angel. Once my Barbies had pretty faces and fits again to match their tiny waistses, I set them up with my toy soldiers, who guarded and protected their houses and hearts. It was like my version of *The Bodyguard* starring the inimitable Whitney Houston. Even though my Barbies were Amazon goddesses and my soldiers skinny little toothpicks, they coupled off and fell in love and I threw them lavish weddings. This is when I realized, Oh my God, tall women can be with short men as well because they're like strong little soldiers, periodt. That was a cute little lesson that I learned.

It became an everyday thing: me driving my toy truck to the marketplace with my squad of sequined Barbies riding shotgun. We'd park at my auntie's stall, and I was just that kid with his electric car and Barbies. That's how I grew up. No one was like, "Oh my God, look at that gay kid with his fuckin' Barbies in the car." First of all, *your* kids don't have a motherfuckin' car, let alone a motherfuckin' Barbie, bitch. So for you to run your mouth, look at your kids, wut da fuk? That's what I would have said if they had said anything. Trust me. But again, the whole town was very accepting.

Now where was I? Oh right, yes, I don't want anyone to shed a tear for me when my mom left. I knew she still loved me (the most, duh). My parents were business-savvy people, and they decided she'd move to America to make more money for our family while my dad stayed behind in the Philippines to run her stall at the market in addition to Twin Bros Transportation. So butch. My mom's goal was to get the rest of our family set up in America, get a green card, then bring me and my dad over to join them all in paradise as soon as possible.

Slight hitch in the plan: my mom didn't trust my dad not to cheat (as I've mentioned, he had a reputation around town as a babaero, English translation: *zaddy*) so I was picked to stay behind, and I guess be a cockblock? It made sense that they chose little ol' me, the middle child, the favorite, to keep my dad company. Before Princess and I were born, my parents were having a tough relationship. My dad was at the peak of a rough patch with drugs and fighting. He didn't really straighten out and fix things with his parents and the rest of his family until right before I was born. My brother, Edwin Jr. ("J.R."), is twelve years older than me, and he was kinda teen angsty, after having a rougher childhood than me and my sister, Princess Mae, two years younger than me, who was still a baby and way too much work to be left behind with a hardworking man.

That toy truck was meant to distract me from my mom and siblings leaving and it worked. After my mom got to Hawaii, she also sent me balikbayan ("coming home") boxes, aka OFW (Overseas Filipino Workers) boxes, once a month. There are ten million Filipinos all over the world, and one of our traditional ways of staying connected while being thousands of miles away is to send special packages home filled with treats, sweets, tinned goods, toys, and other tchotchkes. I read somewhere that we send seven million OFW boxes every year back to the Philippines. It's our way of showing love even when we're apart.

33

My OFW made it feel like Christmas (you'll remember, our favorite holiday) once a month. Mine were mostly filled with junk my mom got from swap meets, like a broken McDonald's Happy Meal toy from the 1980s or a used Winnie the Pooh Halloween costume. I especially loved the thrifted clothes my mom sent, which to me smelled fruity and delicious, like how I imagined Hawaii smelled. I mean, I was a kid who grew up in a town where literally everything smelled like sewage and chicken shit. So secondhand clothes never smelled like mothballs to me—they smelled like a new wardrobe. They were luxury.

I honestly still don't have any resentment toward my mom for leaving or having to do what she had to do, which was work to take care of us. My mom's gonna kill me for saying this, but she always worked so much while we all lived together in the compound that I barely saw her before she left anyway. Truth is, my aunties and my grandma took care of me when I was little, and they were the ones I was really close to, growing up. After my mom gave birth to me, she handed me off to them and said, "Somebody's gotta feed this kid," so they even fuckin' breastfed me.

I've hung out and identified with women my whole entire life, which is probably why I've always felt my femme side so strongly. The aunties on my mom's side have bad-bitch energy vibes: they're strong-minded alpha females and femme fatales. If their husbands ever died, I'd know they killed them. I grew up around that power, and that's why I don't let bitches tell me shit.

I know I sound like a broken record at this point, but my aunties were also always so accepting of my gayness. They also knew from the get-go that I was an entertainer and they loved to make me perform like a court jester. They'd put on girlie songs, dance around, and shout, "Bretman, dance like this!" and I would dance just like them. I was always celebrated. I always talk about them with a smile on my face, and I know, to this day, that when my aunties talk about me, they talk about me with smiles on their faces. They're also annoying as hell sometimes, but anyhoo . . .

Without my mom around, I chilled with my aunties for sure, but my dad and I also grew close, as inseparable as tuna and mayo. We were together so much, people started calling me Junior, even though I wasn't technically the Junior.

Being my dad's sidekick is probably the part I'm fondest of when I think about my childhood. Let me tell you, we were always chopping the block in our trike, looking for adventure. Every fall, this specific tree beetle came around. My dad and I'd go out riding at night with a big-ass stick and shake the trees in our neighbors' yards really hard, so that the bugs would fall out. It was my job to collect and separate the brown (abal-abal) from the black ones (arroz-arroz)—the brown ones tasted better, but you could also fry and eat the black ones if you took off their wings. A little salt and chili, and they were spicy and yummy. Yes, bitch, we ate tree bugs. That's why I'm so experimental with what I put in my mouth today. I'd never turn any food down. I will always try everything once. (Just not vagina. I'm no vagitarian. That's one thing I'm certain of.)

There was never a dull moment any time I was with my dad. We always had something to do, whether it was foraging for the plants you can eat in the jungle or watching football, which I hated. (Luckily, he didn't make me play sports with balls.) He was okay with me being gay, but he was not okay with me being lazy or inactive, so he'd always keep us on the move—I'm still a runner today because he would take me on long runs through the countryside before I even learned how to tie my own shoelaces. Every night we sprinted to the local cemetery and back in the pitch-dark. My dad's beloved dog Blazer would usually chase us from behind, but one time we didn't know he had followed us again, and he got run over by a car. My dad planned an elaborate funeral for Blazer, like a three-day-long open casket memorial. That was the first time I ever saw my dad, also a Leo, cry. Leos never cry, so it was so dramatic. (Btw, Blazer was the inspiration behind the name of my favorite chicken, Blazie, who sadly went missing during the pandemic and is probably now in chicken heaven, strutting around pecking all the other chickens into submission.)

My dad was such an animal lover. We had chickens, quails, pigeons, three pigs, two Chihuahuas, and a big-ass fucking fish. (I would also stay an animal lover—now I have four dogs, Kym the Peacock, a parakeet, Ula the giant Sulcata tortoise, and four cats.) I was in charge of taking care of the chicks and quails, wetting their food and harvesting their eggs. My dad told me once it was his dream to be a vet, which is why it confused me that he was so into cockfighting . . . girl, that was so traumatizing. I went to a few fights, and they were so bloody and violent, and people would be crying over their chickens and sewing up their cuts like they were Conor McGregor (I only know who he is because he posts pics in tighty-whities). I was like, Hey, cockfighters, I'll be outside. Bitch, I'd rather stay home with my grandma and play with her blush. My grandma was so much more fun—the only reason I wanted to go to those cockfights those few times was to collect feathers to make dresses for my Barbies. The sacrifices one has to make for fashion!

The cockfights could also get kinda dangerous, and were not the most appropriate place for a beautiful little angel like myself. My grandma stopped letting me go when someone's cock died, and the fight turned into World War III until the police showed up. My dad also got stabbed a bunch of times at the fights—once by an angry cockfighter but also once by his own cock. They put blades on the chicken's feet, so when they fight, they legit just stab each other. My dad had been trying to grab his chicken away from his opponent and got sliced by his cock on his arm, which started spurting blood everywhere. On top of that, he then got in a heated argument with whoever the fuk won and got stabbed again, right after he survived being gored by his cock. Legend.

You could call my dad a Renaissance man: he liked the finer things in life but could also get down 'n' dirty. He made weird jokes, like describing his sperm as paint because it splattered everywhere. As a kid, I was just like, What the fuck? But now that's probably why I make so many sexual jokes, too. As I mentioned, he was also a prolific babaero, and to this day, I'm still not sure how many half-siblings I have. At least two that my dad and the rest of my family know of. The actual number remains a mystery.

For years, we did so many dykey activities together, until one day one person changed everything. There was a shop right across the street from our house, particularly infamous for hiring young women. Oh my God, I can't believe I'm putting this out there . . . anyway, my dad went to that shop suspiciously often. Then he hired one of those girls to be our "maid," and next thing I knew, she was living with my dad and me in our two-bedroom house on my mom's family compound. Shockingly enough, she was legal, but it was still kind of gross. My dad just told everyone, "Don't worry, she's a lesbian," and everyone believed him because she U-hauled into

37

our house right away, acted like a top, and wore an ugly gray acid-washed baseball hat, all universal symbols of lesbianism.

When the maid—let's call her Martina—came into the picture, my dad ditched me, and I really only hung out with my grandma, aunties, and cousins from that point on. He only cared about the motherfuckin' maid. One day I was super sick and my dad wouldn't even take me to the doctor. But he would take her ass to the doctor. And he only cooked for her now. If I was really hungry and wanted something, he'd bark, "There's food in the fridge, or go to your auntie's house." I saw all this, and saw them being affectionate, but at that age, I still didn't know anything was up.

It wasn't just me who didn't fully understand my dad had a new woman. My mom was also oblivious, being so far away, but all of my aunties eventually saw through the charade. They didn't know what to do, though—they wanted to protect my mom, but they couldn't prove anything, so they kept quiet. Now this is where I came into play.

So it was just the three of us—me, my dad, and Martina the Maid—in our two-bedroom home. I always slept in the middle of the bed I shared with both of them, but somehow always woke up at the foot of the bed or outside in the living room. (But tell me why we would all still bother sleeping in the same bed?) One time I actually did see them having sex. I tried to erase those images in my head because I saw them so young. Kids in America get the whole stork baby talk first to ease the blow, but I saw where I came from and how I was made with my own two eyes, way too soon. It was truly the first time I was like, "Wow, I don't like vaginas."

My dad probably thought that, at six, I was still too young to even comprehend the situation. But I understood more than I wanted to. One day my mom called my dad and he handed me the phone. "Uh, your mom wants to talk to you."

I took the phone and went outside.

"How's the maid?" my mom asked.

Not knowing what the fuck I was telling her, I vomited it all out. How the maid slept with us. How they were always kissing and hugging and giving each other massages. All the dirty details. After I finally stopped talking, I'll never forget how sad my mom's voice got. I could literally hear her heart drop and shatter over the phone. I still feel the pain of my words like it happened yesterday. It was only when I told her that I fully understood that dad's behavior was wrong.

I gave the phone back to my dad, and he and my mom had a nice conversation, like everything was fine and fuckin' dandy. But remember, my mom's a Scorpio. She was already plotting.

After the cat was out of the bag, I distinctly remember one of my aunties questioning me about my dad and Martina, and at some point saying, "I feel like I'm going to throw up," after all the details they didn't know about came out. Then all my aunties banded together and collected money for an airline ticket for my mom to fly back to the Philippines.

My parents proceeded to have the bitchiest catfight over me in court, and my mom and aunties and the court therapist made me memorize dates and events to say to the judge, but I didn't even know how to read yet. I still get sweaty just thinking about this time in my life. It really contributed a lot to fucking up my mental health for a long time. Things came out of my mouth that should not be coming out of a six-year-old's mouth. Like that I saw my dad spit on my mom, or having to describe my dad's sexcapades with the maid.

Ultimately my mom won, and we got the papers for me to come to America. It didn't feel like a win to me, because I felt like I'd well and truly lost my dad. I was so scarred. Imagine this man being your hero, and spending your whole childhood wanting to be this man, until he hurts the only woman you will ever probably love. I felt grossed out with all guys after that.

It was actually all too easy for me to transition from having a dad to not having a dad, because at the exact same time everything was happening, my dad cut his hair. He literally stopped looking like my dad. I remember being so sad about his short hair. All the boys on his side of the family had long, luscious locks they were very proud of, and I felt like the haircut was the universe telling me, "Girl, the dad you thought you had is gone." We would never be as close again.

Unfortunately, the only person I wanted to hurt after this nightmare ended was myself. As I grew older and became fully conscious of what really went down between my parents, the blame shifted from my dad being the evil one. I started to yell at myself out loud, like, "My family would still be together if you never told your mom, you loud-ass bitch." I spent the rest of my childhood telling myself it was my fault, and it's hard to erase what you tell yourself when you're a kid. So many things affected my personality after my parents split, good and bad. Their separation drove me to want to be the breadwinner of my family, because I wanted to be greater than my dad, and become the dad my dad would never be for my little sister. And I felt guilty that my mom was now alone, and that it all started because of me, and started acting like her wife, which is probably another reason why I'm so fucking gay.

40

But that trauma all took a little more time to really settle in, and even more time for me to really process. All I knew immediately after the court case was that I was on my way to Hawaii, and I'd get to see my favorite cousins Keiffer and Colin, who'd already moved to America a few months ahead of me, again. Before the flight, I stuffed my backpack full of sweets from the sari-sari store, because I was scared that America wouldn't have good candy, and the whole way there I couldn't sit still and kept pressing all the buttons. My mom was like "Staaahp," but I was just so excited I couldn't.

I didn't know what I was excited for—I barely even knew what America was. Before I left, my aunties kept telling me, "Oh, bring me a boyfriend!" even though they all had full-on husbands. I guess I thought there were lots of hot guys in America? That sounded promising, but I was also just curious about white people in general because I didn't see them growing up. I was always surrounded by people who looked like me, Aeta, or the paler Filipinos on TV. In my head, every white person was a celebrity.

Even more than white people, I was super excited to try McDonald's, which was considered fine dining back in the Philippines. Oooh, girl, and Dunkin' Donuts. I know, bitch, she's not even that good, but at the time DD was in her prime in the Philippines, selling doughnuts on a stick. You could only get them in Manila, our capital, though, six hours away. I saw the commercial for those doughnuts a million times and wanted one so bad. (Up to that point, the only sticks I had gotten to hold were the ones I threw at people covered in my poo.)

Right before we landed, everyone put their window shades up, and I almost broke my neck trying to take in all of Oahu, my new home, from the air. It was drizzling, but the sun was also out. It was so poetically beautiful, I almost feel like I could write a poem about it, but I'm not going to, yeah. In the Philippines, everything is green or gray. Hawaii was the coolest shade of orange I'd ever seen—it looked like the whole island had the best and brightest. In Hawaii, it felt like the rainbow was within reach, you could see where it started and ended. Like you could practically kiss the leprechaun with his pot of gold.

After we landed, I couldn't wait to get lei'd for the first time—my mom used to put plumeria necklaces in my OFW boxes. I didn't, but my uncle Lucifer picked us up at the airport and I was blown away by his car, a broken-down white 1990 Toyota 4Runner. Seeing a car out on the streets back home had been so rare. When it happened, all the kids would form a circle around it, press our grimy hands all over it, then pile on top of it and not let go until the owner sped off and we all fell off onto the gravel.

Girl, on the ride from the airport, I stuck my head out the window and inhaled deeply. This is going to sound weird, but to me, America smelled like Irish Spring soap. Fresh and clean. My mom also put Irish Springs in my OFW boxes—it wasn't until much later that I found out it's the cheapest soap you can get at Rite Aid, and is what a truck stop smells like. But that day, Hawaii smelled like Irish Spring, which smelled like pure luxury.

I was in awe of how clean everything was, and the green road signs telling everyone where to go. I was so excited, eating chips and taking in the blissful scenery—mossy green mountaintops perched above the sapphire blue water. It was fucking paradise. Which is why I don't know what came over me when I threw the potato-chip bag out the window. My uncle was livid. "We don't do that in America!" he scolded. "That's littering! Don't throw trash out the window. This is not the Philippines. Do you see trash in the road?"

Our first stop was Burger King, and I could not believe that I was getting to eat fast food, plus they had a motherfucking playground WITH A BALL PIT. The playground smelled like puke, but I kept going outside and playing on it anyway. I was in disbelief that I was in America, surely the most magical place on earth. It was euphoric, almost a dream.

I still see Hawaii pretty much how I saw it that very first day from the plane: beautiful and peaceful. I still geek out about living on such a tiny island. It feels like a kingdom, and I feel like motherfuckin' royalty every day I'm blessed to be here.

How to Handle Family Drama

If I could go back in a time machine, here's what I'd tell baby Bret after he went through those traumatic, toxic times:

1. **Stay calm.**

    It's hard not to react when people are freaking out, but it doesn't help the situation if you wig out in the moment, too. That just escalates an already explosive situation.

2. **Talk to people you trust.**

    Just because you saw something happen, that doesn't mean you have to deal with it yourself, especially when you're a kid. Find someone you trust who can help you figure out what the best next step should be.

3. **It's all right to cry.**

    I think my go-to emotion then was stoic, stunned silence. You know what tho, bottling shit up inside is never healthy. Let the emotion out, even if people around you shame you for showing emotions. Give yourself permission to cry—I wish I had.

4. **Ask for counseling.**

   Even better if you can talk about what's going on with a trained professional. I wish I hadn't been so scarred by that court-appointed counselor then. A lot of cultures look down on seeing a shrink and think it's weak, but there's absolutely no shame in getting real help.

5. **Channel your sadness into a healthy activity.**

   Being a joiner in so many clubs and sports after I moved to America would save my sanity. It got me thinking more about other things than about myself and my guilt, and it introduced me to friends who could listen, and who shared similar experiences.

FOUR

Island Girl

I felt like I had made it in life on that drive back from the airport, and I was only fucking seven. Oh my God, I thought, I'm in Hawaii, I'm rich. Then we got to my new house in Oahu, and I moved in with twenty-five family members.

When I first moved in, I was excited, thinking we lived in a mansion because it had five bedrooms. Then it hit me pretty quickly that our living arrangement wasn't exactly "normal" in America. We weren't rich. Far from it. Nobody else (that I could see) had five families crammed into one house. In the Philippines, our whole extended family lived together, but we were spread out on our property in separate houses. We weren't on top of each other.

I would now be sharing one domicile with my other grandma, Inang, my mom, her two brothers, her sister, their spouses, and all twelve of their children, including Keiffer and Colin. Basically, four of Grandma Inang's eight children now lived together under one roof. My immediate family had to pile into one bedroom with my grandma. I was like, Girl! That bitch got a bed to herself, my mom and sister, Princess Mae, shared a bed, and my brother slept on the patio. I think I had PTSD from sharing a bed with my dad and his hat-wearing mistress, so I took the floor, thank you very much (and to this day I love sleeping on the floor, even though I have a fancy-ass four-poster bed now).

It was an adjustment living with my siblings again after four years. I barely knew them. My brother, J.R., was nineteen years old by this point, and wanted nothing to do with me. Princess, who was about five years old now, made it very clear she was the boss of the house and was so possessive of her belongings, like, "Do not touch my Barbies, bitch."

I was the new girl and got hazed a little bit by Princess and my cousins, who had seniority. Battling for the bathroom was war, and I'd have to wrestle a bitch if I wanted to watch *Hannah Montana*. Our house had three TVs: my grandma got her own, the adults got another, and the kids had the last one. I had to watch a lot of *Robot Chicken*, WWE, and other sports—there were a lot of straight people in my house (emphasis on *straight* in a derogatory way, *kiss-kiss*) who enjoyed watching people shoot or kick a ball and run back and forth, over and over again, day in and day out.

If I wanted any alone time, I'd hang out on the roof until I got in trouble. My uncle Lucifer was so strict (remember the chip bag?), and he made my life a living hell. He owned the house, and when he got home from work every day, everybody—kids and adults—would turn the TV and the lights off and scurry like cockroaches back into our rooms to hide, afraid he'd find something to criticize about us. He acted like we all owed him for the house, even though every single person worked hard and helped pay the mortgage.

You shouldn't be scared of your own family. You should be able to say no to your uncle, especially if you don't want to scratch his fucking back with a credit card, which I only did because I knew he would tell my mom that I was a lazy bitch if I didn't, and my mom would scold me. Uncle Lucifer had pimples on his back, and I literally loved scraping that shit fucking hard enough to pop them (which he hated). One day I got a little too comfy, and I popped them a little too hard. He shouldered my elbow. Then he asked me to get him a cup of water. I went to the kitchen, grabbed a cup, opened the motherfucking toilet bowl, dunked it in, brought that cup of toilet water to him, and said, "Here you go." I watched him drink every fucking ounce. Then I kept scraping his back, while feeling so good. I was like, Sis, you shouldered me, but I'm gonna shoulder your insides. Oh, and this is T-motherfucking-M-I, but you know where he had found me right before he asked me to scratch his back? In the bathroom, taking a shit.

Despite how it might sound, living in that house did become such a happy time of my life. I would not trade my childhood for any other—it molded and shaped little Bretman into the fine young womyn you see today. I was never bored, because my cousins were there all the time, and we got so close that I don't even see them as my cousins anymore. I love them like they're my siblings.

My mom's two other brothers, my strong uncles Bobot and George, stood in for my dad when I was growing up, and considered me their son. It was so wild because my uncles are such masculine men, but they also never once made me feel like shit for being gay. They just made sure I was always doing my best and putting my best foot forward. "You have to work hard for your mom," they'd tell me. My mom was always at work, so my uncle's wives, my aunties, who were stay-at-homers, cooked for me and raised me, just like my other aunties had back in the Philippines.

Everyone in my house had a big personality and was so plain weird. Like, my cousin Marie was so good at lying, she could say it was the thirty-sixth of July and I'd believe her. She'd tell her dad she was going to the park, then say, "Bret, we're going to my boyfriend's house and I'm gonna pay you five dollars to hang out with his little brother."

Then there's my beautiful grandma Inang, oh my God, and her saggylicious tits. Grandma Inang was a native woman, and that native woman loved to be naked. She never wore a shirt, unless someone was coming over. Every time I think about my grandma, she's not wearing a shirt. I can still picture her putting baby powder under her titties. Flopping them back and to the side, dabbing a little baby powder, then flopping them right back. She loved to let everyone know that she was the reason why all the girls in my family had big boobs. If I was a girl, I would be thanking Grandma Inang for my big boobs as well. I'd always know it was a Sunday when she sat in the living room watching *Wheel of Fortune* on mute. She didn't speak English, so she couldn't read the puzzles . . . so I don't know what the fuh she was doing.

From the outside looking in, so many families and huge personalities living together under one roof was a situation that probably might have freaked people out. But if anyone was hurt, we would all be there for each other, you know what I mean? One thing we all had in common is that we are all tough lovers. You would never hear the phrase "I love you" in my household. No no no. You would never see us hugging in that household. But you would always hear the loudest laughter. And no compliments ever, except backhanded ones. For example, someone might say to me, "You look so nice when your hair is not long. You look like a boy." Or I might say to Keiffer, "You look like you only ate four meals today." That's the household that I grew up in—loud, backhanded-compliment-giving tough lovers.

Keiffer giving me shit while I was growing up is the reason I'm now fluent in three languages. My first week in Hawaii, we got in a big fight because she made fun of me for not being able to speak English. (P.S. Keiffer's pronouns are she/her.) Mind you, Keiffer had only moved to America a few months before I did. She was acting all high and mighty like she was Mrs. America or some ho, and I got so upset about her bragging and teasing that I made it my number one mission in life to speak English better. If there's anything about Bretman Rock, he's always fueled by spite.

So I picked up English really fast, first by watching reality TV shows like *Bad Girls Club, A Shot at Love with Tila Tequila, America's Next Top Model,* and *RuPaul's Drag Race.* I would repeat the judges' critiques and mimic all the badass bitches. If a girl on a show was sad, I was sad. If Tyra screamed, "Be quiet, Tiffany! Be quiet! What is wrong with you? STOP IT. I have never in my life yelled at a girl like this!" then I'd scream, "Be quiet, Tiffany! Be quiet! What is wrong with you? STOP IT. I have never in my life yelled at a girl like this!" When my sister and I got into fights, I'd run into the bathroom and practice what I would say to her when I saw her again. My second language was Reality TV English. Tanisha Thomas from *BGC* taught me how to say "Pop off." Here's a fun fact to imprez your friends: "Hey girl, hey!"

actually originated on *A Shot at Love with Tila Tequila*. You won't learn that in school. I'd be standing in front of the mirror almost 24/7 pretending I was in a booth doing my own confessionals. "Like, can y'all believe Princess acted like that today?" I'd say into my mirror/camera. Then I'd pause as if a producer was asking me a follow-up question. "She really did not want to give me twenty dollars."

Once I had my mission of beating Keiffer at English, you could not get that TV remote out of my hand. Especially after I discovered the holy grail—HBO On Demand. Let me explain: I'd never even heard of Beyoncé—shut your mouth, yes it's true—until the afternoon I heard Keiffer singing the magical "To the left, to the left . . ." to another cousin who was watering the lawn. "What is that you're singing?" I asked, all wide-eyed. Keiffer wasn't even a good singer, but I knew a hit when I heard one.

"You don't know Beyoncé?"

I pretended like I did, but it was too clear I was lying. Keiffer marched me into the house and found a Beyoncé concert on HBO On Demand. I've never been the same since. After that, we played every Beyoncé, Britney, and Lady Gaga music video ever made 6,543 times over. I would get so excited to listen to Ciara's "1, 2 Step," and then fell madly deeply in love with Shakira. That's all we'd play in my house when it was cleaning day. Eight a.m., boogers still in my eyes, I knew it was time to do the laundry when I heard her belting in her signature thick contralto yodel.

There was RiRi and Mariah and Xtina and Alicia. "Oh my God, all these girls!" I cried to myself. "So many options!" HBO On Demand was like opening Pandora's box. If I'd wanted to listen to music in the Philippines, my dad had to burn it on a CD for me. And the only girl he'd ever played for me was the chick from

Blondie. There was no going back to Debbie Harry after I saw the likes of Beyoncé and these other bad bitches.

Although I did have to take one long hiatus from HBO On Demand one time when I accidentally paid for one of the pay-per-views. My mom got so mad with me that day I had to take a break from TV. This might have been the time when I discovered the luxury of reading. Again, when I learned how to read, there was no stopping me. I inhaled *Diary of a Wimpy Kid, Junie B. Jones*, and *Goosebumps*. Divas of the written word, bitch.

Not long after I got to Hawaii, everybody started to notice how I'd picked up English so well, low-key quicker than Keiffer and Colin. You know, if Keiffer had not made it into a competition and motherfucking said some smart shit, I really would not have discovered Beyoncé *and* started reading. If Keiffer had just left me the fuck alone, I would probably still be illiterate and not the confident woman I am today. Thank God she didn't.

2011 Christmas party at my cousins'

My cousins, my sisters, and I became a wolf pack. We always had each other's backs. With so many people around, I never ran out of things to do, like twerking on my uncle Bobot. I lived for our weekly family excursions to Star Markets, where I could play the claw crane machine, the coolest thing I'd ever seen. I was always so excited to win fucking fake jewelry and plushie toys, I'd almost pee in my pants on the way there. And don't get me started when I found out Chuck E. Cheese existed!

However, you can't play the crane game or go to Chuck E. Cheese if you don't have any money. And you can't buy yourself shit at the local swap meets with no pesos. There were certain luxuries we had in the Philippines that we couldn't afford here. Even if I was still getting my allowance of five pesos a day, they probably wouldn't have gotten me much in America. My mom had basically become a pro thrifter after she moved to Hawaii so that she could send clothes and OFW boxes back to her relatives in the Philippines. The first time we went, I just asked my mom for some cash, and she gave me $20. (It was really more like $10, but the way she went on and on about it, it was like she gave me $20 . . . what was that gonna get me, girl?) I wound up buying a guinea pig but didn't realize until I brought her home that the bitch was pregnant. She gave birth to three kids, and those three kids would eventually multiply to thirty-six. At that point, I realized that I had to get rid of all these guinea pigs, especially after they ate all the grass in the backyard. I knew if my uncle Lucifer saw those bare-ass patches, he was gonna kill me.

And then my first real business was born . . . out of necessity, and because I just couldn't keep showing up at those swap meets broke. I was so stressed out about my thirty-six guinea pigs—worrying that my uncle would murder me, or that we'd get deported. Even though we were all here legally, if we got in trouble with the law we could still get shipped back home, and I didn't know what the laws were around how many guinea pigs you could have. That's what was going in my head while I was hiding all thirty-six of them.

I started selling guinea pigs on Craigslist. My cousin introduced me to Craigslist because he bought and sold used cell phones. He always met his "clients" at Burger King and let me come with him. It was all a little shady but felt like the coolest thing in the world to me. For my guinea pig biz, I went from charging $25 for one to just basically handing them out left and right for $5 after I realized I had to lower my prices to make money—it was the simple concept of supply and demand.

Girl, I really took it seriously. I did a bunch of research on the breeds and came up with an ingenious plan—I'd charge $5 for guinea pigs with one color, $15 for pigs with two colors, and three, well, I'll see if I even want to sell them to you, bitch. Suddenly everybody wanted my exotic tricolor guineas, even though I pulled the buzz for them completely out of my ass.

By the end of the summer I'd made $600 off of the guinea pigs, enough to pay back my uncle for the patches in the grass, plus more than enough to spoil myself silly at swap meets on the weekends. I always started off my swap meet days out at the Filipino food carts set up at the meet—I couldn't be shopping on an empty stomach. I'd get lumpia and a neon-orange soup called miki. As a young kid, I wasn't really into shopping for clothes yet—mainly gadgets and science kits, beakers, crystals, and magnifying glasses. I liked to use them to mix things together and make my own concoctions and formulas for face masks. Also, I'd gotten got sucked into the vortex of science YouTube videos and became obsessed with blowing things up myself. I loved that guy Steve Spangler who always went on *Ellen* and blew things up. I wanted to make things explode, too. At the swap meets, I had a talent for stretching $10. I came home with bags and bags of shit because I would not leave the sellers alone until they gave me a discount. The other cool thing is that when I shopped for Barbies, I never got weird looks; I always got friendly smiles.

I didn't just use the money I earned at swap meets—as soon as I had some money I also made a beeline for McDonald's. I dressed up in my finest the first time I went to eat there. I'll never forget my first McDonald's oufit—denim overalls with no shirt on underneath and one strap dangling down so I could serve shoulder—and my first order: ten-piece chicken McNuggets, a Happy Meal with a cheeseburger and fries, Powerade, and peach pie for dessert. I also got a Hello Kitty watch from the Happy Meal, bitch.

My entrepreneurial skills continued to blossom after that first guinea pig windfall. When I went to Costco with my mom, I was allowed to buy one thing per trip, so of course I bought gummy bears. Then when school started, I sold Ziploc baggies of them, sprinkled with plum seasoning, for $1. I had seen other kids selling gummies on the playground, but I busted into that market anyway—I've always had an innate ability to spot weakness and pounce. I knew I had to be the best gummy seller in the game. And I was—my plum-topped gummies were so popular, everybody would be looking for me at recess. Bitches knew that every time Bretman Sacayanan arrived on the playground with his satchel, he'd have a fresh batch of prime plummy gummies.

Selling plum gummies actually reminded me of another early

job I had back in the Philippines. When I was very small, I used to walk around town after school with a board that had balloons stapled on it. I'd charge one peso for people to pick a number from a bucket. Whatever balloon on my board corresponded with the number they pulled would be the one they got to take home. People loved that game. I was so popular—"Balloon Boy," they called me, and even adults would come chasing after me to play.

Like the balloons, my plummy gummies caught on fast—the demand got too high, actually. It got to the point where I was like, I can't even play tag out here in peace without someone asking for gummies, like, give a bitch some work-life boundaries plz. That's when I realized that while I liked making money, customer service was not for me.

Nevertheless, she persisted. There were cockfights every weekend and even though I'd been traumatized by cockfights when I was younger, I remembered how beautiful chicken feathers were when I used to go and collect them to make my Barbies dresses. I'd go along and then I turned the feathers trimmed off from the cocks, and eventually other bird feathers, into earrings. One dollar for a stack of feathers or $5 for one longer feather from a red-winged blackbird.

Some of my proudest moments as a kid would be going back to my mom and saying, "Look, I doubled the money you gave me!" And she'd say, "Okay, you can give back what I gave you and you can keep what you made." And that, bitches, was how I was taught business.

Between making more money than I'd ever made before and reality TV, I was absolutely loving my new homeland. And Hawaii is so gay, so I fit right in. You can walk around the whole day with gold-tinted eyebrows, and instead of people judging or questioning you, they smile and ask where you got the brow gel.

Everybody around me was also brown or Asian or Filipino. So many people looked like me and spoke Ilocano and Tagalog, but probably also ended up learning how to speak English from *Tila Tequila*, like me.

In all fairness, I know that in saying that Hawaii is my new homeland, I'm part of the problem of immigrants erasing native Hawaiian culture, regardless if I'm not doing it in a malicious way. To try and work against this kind of erasure, I've always tried to teach myself about Native Hawaiian history and culture. One thing I've learned from true Hawaiians is that "Aloha" is so much more than what a tourist's definition of the word is. Yes, it means hello and goodbye and I love you, but it's so much more. The root of Aloha is actually not *alo*—it's *ha*, which means "the breath of life." Back in the day, when Hawaiians would say hello and good-bye, they would touch foreheads and exchange breath.

What's funny then is that the word for white people, *Haole*, comes from the roots *ha*, "breath," and *ole*, "no." The direct translation for Haole is "no breath," because when you're out of breath, you turn white. Imagine, if you will, all of these islanders seeing white voyagers for the very first time, centuries ago, and thinking they were sick or dead because they were so pasty. LOL.

I actually think Filipino culture is very similar to Hawaiian culture. We are both very positive and resourceful. Native Hawaiian culture also worships the land and the water—I learned from season two of my show that the mountains and water here are believed to be siblings, where the eldest takes care of the younger one by watering all the plants on the mountains, and the younger one feeds the eldest when the water runs back down to the sea. Which reminds me of how much we value water and the rice plants in the Philippines, you know, and taking care of them so they could take care of us. And in both cultures, unity and community are so important. Everybody has a job and a role in coming together to create a sense of togetherness.

Something I learned about and relate to so deeply is what Hawaiians call the Aloha spirit. If you really live here, you should understand that *Aloha* is not just a word, it's an energy and an aura that's indescribable, that lives within us. I feel so grounded in Hawaii, in this sense of Aloha. It makes me feel most like a human being when I feel the waves of the South Pacific on my skin, when I can feel so close to the earth, to my family, to my community. I always try to embody that energy, the energy of Hawaii, wherever I go, because it's so kind and positive and hopeful.

The Aloha spirit is everything to me.

How to Start Your Own Business

It's hard to know if you have an idea as potentially lucrative as my chicken feather earring business. I'm not going to write another book on business tips (yet, although I totally could), but here are a few practical tips for the cutest entrepreneurs who might start out as broke as I was:

- Think about doing something you're good at and that has little to no overhead, like crafting, dog walking, fixing cars, or tech support for all the oldies in your life. If you're an MUA like me, set up appointments with your girlfriends before big events.

- Come up with the cutest name for your business. But not too cute. I'll tell you later about how I was stuck with Bretman Rock, Paper, Scissors, LLC for years . . .

- Put in 150 percent and see if you're still into it. If you're having fun and you don't even know how much time has gone by when you're working on something, that shows that you're passionate.

- Lean on your community. One thing that I love about Filipinos so much is that we really do genuinely bring each other up. And that reflects especially in my work today—Asians and Filipinos have all gotten me where I am now. People always like helping out young people with a dream and drive.

- Most important, don't get high on your own supply. Like, I would never have had any profit whatsoever if I ate all of my gummy bears with plum seasoning, or if I'd gotten grounded for life after thirty-six guinea pigs tore up the yard.

FIVE

A Bad Bitch
in School

No one knows this: Walmart was the birthplace of the reality star Bretman Rock. This is *not* a branded content chapter, this a true story, so pay attention and take notes. There will be a quiz at the end, yeah.

Before my very first day of second grade in Hawaii, which was actually the first day of second quarter, we got a shopping list. My mom read the list out loud, and I was shocked, like, What the hell is half of this? What do you mean, I need kids' scissors *and* a pair of sharp scissors? Notebooks, index cards, highlighters, compass, eraser, Wite-Out, binder, glue stick, Ziploc-motherfuckin-bags, calculator, graph paper, crayons and colored pencils and Sharpies and a Cray-Pas. What the fuck is a Cray-Pas?

In the Philippines I only needed a pen and a piece of paper

and a bag. And I already told you that my mom and dad sold school supplies, so I thought I knew what was up. Now I was confused. Why did I need eight rolls of toilet paper and Kleenex and paper towels? Was I moving into the school building?

Whatever, I knew I couldn't show up on my first day empty-handed looking weak, so my mom, my cousins, and I headed to Walmart. And oh my God when I tell you—when I walked through those automatic doors and saw the security cameras facing me and a TV monitor showing me sashaying in, seeing myself on that screen was one of the biggest, most defining moments of my life.

We had malls in the Philippines, and they had cameras, but they didn't have live footage of you that you could see yourself in. This was different. I was geeking out in front of those Walmart security cameras while none of the other shoppers looked twice. I hadn't even come across phones that had cameras in them yet! You know what I mean? So to see myself live on video for the first time, that was a big deal at that point. It was so dramatic. I thought that being on video meant that the *world* was seeing me for the first time. For someone who grew up wanting to be the center of attention and knowing that I deserved to be the center of attention, this moment of truly knowing I was being watched and filmed was such an awakening. That was the exact moment when I really realized: *This is where I belong.* In front of a camera. And Walmart was the birthplace of my essence.

I really thought I was finally on *Big Brother.* This was so much better than pretending to be in a confessional in front of my bath-room mirror at home. I spent the rest of the shopping trip walking around the store like I was being watched the whole time. "These cabbages are looking at me funny," I said out loud as I walked. "I don't know why they're looking at me like that. I'm sending them home." Mind you, my cousins were still in the school supplies aisle, looking for rulers and plastic pocket folders. I didn't even end up looking for school supplies that day because I was just hunting for every possible camera angle in the store.

I wasn't nervous about starting school in a new country—I was more concerned about how I was gonna carry an entire office supplies catalog to school. Imagine this ninety-five-pound second grader with a giant backpack and two Walmart bags in his hands giddily walking down the street. I swear to God, it was the same vibe as when SpongeBob sang, "I'm ready, I'm ready, I'm ready, I'm ready!" I was beyond excited carrying my bags and my toilet paper.

I had to be there at eight, but I was fashionably late, duh (even though school was only a three-minute walk from home). When I walked into Ms. Silva's class at 8:30 a.m., I was *thee* new girl, and when I tell you, Zooey Deschanel could never. I felt so damn important. I broke everybody's neck that day—all the second graders turned around to check out the new blood.

I guess you could say I came there to make friends, yeah, even though I knew everybody knew each other already. I didn't even give a shit that I barely spoke English. (This was still before Keiffer had bullied me about it.) When I first moved here, I knew the basics like *yes, no, my name is, good morning.* Two very excited girls came up to me that first day, and I'm still besties with them today. One of them, Khrizza, was the first person at school to say a word to me. She asked me if I was Filipino, and I said very quietly (probably the only time in my life I've ever said anything quietly), "Yuh."

"I'm Filipino," she said, smiling. "Do you want to sit with me and Laura?"

That's when I was like, Oh my God, all these bitches want to be my friend already! It was so opposite of the American high school movies I'd watched back in the Philippines, where the first day you have to eat lunch in the bathroom and people are throwing spitballs at you. I was like, Girl, this is not what they sold me in *Mean Girls*, but I'll take it. (Okay, I hadn't watched *Mean Girls* at that point.)

Almost all of the kids at my school were brown, Pacific Islander, or Asian. I felt like I fit in right away. People didn't know what the fuck I was saying, but I was instantly that funny kid who was friends with all the girls. At first all of the guys wanted to be my friend, too (more on how that changed in the next chapter . . .), but I didn't want to play tag with them—I'd rather build sandcastles with the girls. I was a real Mr./Mrs. Aloha, even if you wouldn't have known it by looking at me because of my resting bitch face. I still hate that I have a resting bitch face. I always look like I hate everyone in the world, and it's not true! Anyway, I made so many lovely friends, every color of the rainbow. I always felt like a local celebrity. I was literally the only gay kid in my school (I had to bring some culture to them stat, so I made them watch *RuPaul's Drag Race*). I stood out, but I was also cherished by most people for that reason.

At one point I was part of a group called BBLKAT (pronounced Bubba-Lak-Atah). It was all our initials: Bretman Britney Laura Khrizza Abigail Trixie. We actually had two names we voted on, BBLKAT or Fridge Attack, because, poor Britney, every day after school we went to her house and attacked her muthafuckin' fridge. Every time, Britney would get in trouble with her parents, like, "Why do your friends eat all our food?" (But now that I think about it, like, Why did you keep letting her invite us, knowing full

Me and my bitches

well we were going to eat all your motherfucking food? Seems like a you problem.) Most of my friends' parents loved me too, while my mom hated all my friends, but she's a Scorpio, that's just how she's built. After I got into makeup in middle school, my friends' moms would always ask me to put their makeup on for them. They thought I was a good influence on their little angels, but little did they know, when we got a little older, I'd open a hickey cover-up business. Every girl who had a purple love bite on her neck and was afraid to go home would know I was the go-to to help them. (At one point, I was making $50 a week from my hickey cover-up biz!)

From the moment I got to America, all my cousins and aunties told my mom I was the smart one, and that I was going to be the (mer)man of the house. "This is going to be the kid that's gonna be a doctor," they said, not giving one fuck if my brother or sister was in the same room. "Bretman is your breadwinner."

I hated school when I was a kid in the Philippines, mostly because in the Philippines the teachers were allowed to hit you. I was also, for lack of a better word, a relatively spoiled brat back home. My cousins who babysat literally washed me in bed with a cloth, you know? If I didn't feel like going to school, my dad wouldn't care and I'd just hang out with him. When I moved to America, my mom started to really enforce my going to school. And I didn't mind. I was so grateful to come to America, and I was just like, You know what? I'm going to prove them all right. I'm going to be the smartest one and I am going to be my mom's breadwinner. After that fashionably late first day, I started going to school early. Every day I was the first one out of all of my cousins to wake up and get into that shower.

I learned to love school for so many reasons. First of all, it was so easy. Since I was held back a grade when I arrived in America, I was older than everybody in second grade, so I already knew cursive and multiplication. I struggled with English at first, but I was immediately the smartest bitch in science, and even more so in math, because there's no language barrier when it comes to numbers.

School was fun because it gave me things to do, and got me out of the house I shared with my whole immediate family. I was a total joiner from the get-go, all the way through the end of high school. In elementary school I was a junior police officer, the pretty girl who held up the stop sign so bitches could cross the street without getting run over. I also became a peer helper so that I could wear a bright yellow vest and everyone had to look at me. I carried a clipboard at recess and reported kids who were not using the jungle gym equipment ethically or efficiently. Peer helpers heard all the kids' stupid-ass problems and snitched on other kids, like, "Divina doesn't want to share her snack," which was then recorded and processed by us. Now don't get it twisted; even though I heard the snitches out, I was still Mr. Aloha—when I walked to school, all of my elementary school friends would scream my name, like I was Beyoncé on the red carpet and they were paparazzi. Basically school was my very first experience with being an influencer.

School gave me the audience I realized I'd wanted since that moment at Walmart, since I started watching reality TV . . . my whole life, actually. Through elementary school I thought that meant that I wanted to be an actor. In third grade, I was cast in my first acting gig, the starring role of Genie in a school production of *Aladdin*. My very first line, as I emerged from my lamp, was supposed to be a simple "Ta-dah, that's me!" But I felt it needed a little rewrite. Let's just say that I was a method actor. So I zhoozhed it up a little, singsonging it like, "TA-DAH, that's me!" with some spicy neck moves and talk-to-the-hand motions. If I remember correctly, I ended it all with a dramatic finger snap.

"Bretman, c'mon, just go 'Ta-dah, that's me,'" the director begged.

I refused to say it like that. It was a flashy role, and she obviously gave it to me for a reason. She knew how passionate I'd be about it! Let's just say we had our creative differences, and that to this day, I still won't shut the fuck up about my turn as the lovable, larger-than-life Genie. That's the first thing that's going to be on my IMDB account. *Aladdin* in third grade. Thank you very much.

My middle school ID—you better recognize her

In middle school I joined what we called "leadership," which was basically student council. I only joined because you had to be in it in order to do the talent show. Them's were the rules, no matter how random. I know you didn't ask about what I did for the talent show, but I'm gonna tell you anyway. I choreographed a Britney Spears medley and remixed it myself (I still remember the first two moves). And you know, me being the being the bad-ass thoughtful bitch that I am, I hired my peers who were also in student leadership who unfortunately didn't have the talent that I did as backup dancers, and I paid them in grades because we got an A for our performance. Did we get a standing ovation for that A performance from our peers? Yes, we did.

My other masterpiece was choreographing Britney and Khrizza's song-and-dance routine to Miley Cyrus's "Best of Both Worlds." I had to let the girls have their moments, too, yeah. I could be the diva *and* their stage mom!

Oh, I almost forgot my most important activity—I was the star of the student-run TV station ILIMA TV in middle school. This was the next step, you know, going from closed-circuit TV monitors at Walmart to finally having a real audience of my own, and nobody had a choice but to watch me tell them what was for lunch.

Of course I added my own flair. I dubbed myself "Bretney Spears," and this is a sample of how I would do it: "Hey guys, good morning, it's Bretney. Today is June thirtieth and for lunch we will be having Kalua pork. I know you wanted pizza, but . . . bitch, that is not pizza, it's cheese and cardboard, yuh. So line up."

Okay, I definitely couldn't say "bitch." I was the teacher's pet, so I didn't want to ruffle any feathers. And all of my teachers were so accepting of me. My PE teachers even let me pick if I wanted to be on the boys' or girls' teams. (Before you get your granny panties in a knot, I mean, if we were playing football, I wasn't going to be on the girls' team and tackle them, duh. But I was all over the girls' badminton, a no-contact sport.)

I want to give a shout-out to my girl teachers in particular (Hi, Ms. Silva and Ms. Alimaza!), the first people who ever told me that I had star quality. They knew Bretman Rock before Bretman Rock even knew who he was destined to be.

At the end of sixth grade, I had a teacher named Mrs. Matsumur who wrote each of her students a letter. After graduation practice, we all came back to our homes and found our letters on our tables. I opened mine and was immediately in my feels. It was all about how much she believed in me. How bright I was and that everything I wanted to do in life I was going to achieve. She ended it by saying, "Continue on your path to success. I know that someday you will be the actor that you dream to be. Reach for the stars and you will be one. You are one."

I cried so much.

To this day, I've kept a folder with all of my achievements going all the way back to elementary school. Yes, I have the receipts. All of my test results, report cards, honor roll notifications, perfect attendance records (elementary and middle school only, bishes, that was a different Bret), hard worker badges, along with a bronze trophy from the mathematics awards. I'm just so proud of these. I'll probably have them until the day I die.

When I was in the Philippines, I didn't know that my mom and her siblings were living on top of each other in Hawaii. Even though they all worked at a hotel, at one point, four of the families were living in my uncle and auntie's garage. Their beds were literally made out of their clothes that they piled up to sleep on. When I first arrived, it was a huge wake-up call. My family was not living the lavish lifestyle that I thought they would be in America.

All immigrants hear about the American Dream—that in America, the world is your oyster, bitch. As soon as my plane touched down, I remember thinking, *I'm in America now. I can be anybody. I have no excuse.* My American Dream has only ever looked like hard work. I barely even saw my mom because she had two jobs, as a hostess/cook at a military base restaurant and selling vegetables in Chinatown. And even though my dad was a cheater, I knew he was a man who worked hard for everything he had.

I always knew I was going to be a star (and not the doctor my family thought I'd be), the breadwinner of my family, but I also knew that it was gonna take so much work and so many sacrifices. That I, like everyone else in my family, had to give it my all to get everything.

70

And all of these experiences, besties, are what make up my backbone and my foundation, and also explains why I always go above and beyond to have a motherfuckin' outfit to match everything I do.

My Superlatives

MOST LIKELY TO BE MY HIGH SCHOOL YEARBOOK PHOTOGRAPHER BUT ONLY TAKE PICTURES OF MYSELF

MOST LIKELY TO COVET BLACK BUSHY ARMPIT HAIR

MOST LIKELY TO STEAL MY SISTER'S BOYFRIEND . . . 'S T-SHIRTS

MOST LIKELY TO LOOK LIKE A GUY NAMED JOEL

MOST LIKELY TO MAKE ORIGAMI WHILE TAKING A SHIT

MOST LIKELY TO LOSE MY VIRGINITY ON A PILLOW

MOST LIKELY TO LOOK LIKE A MODEL WHILE ASLEEP

MOST LIKELY TO EAT ICE CREAM IN BED

MOST LIKELY TO DIE DOING THE SPLITS

MOST LIKELY TO BUY JELLY BEANS AT ROSS

How to Be the Teacher's Pet Without Everyone Else Hating You

1. Forget an apple—bring them something actually useful, like a Tylenol or Starbucks, if you got money like that.

2. Get personal—ask how their weekend was or bond over your mutual love of graphic prints.

3. Leave them love notes saying, "Don't tell anyone else, but you're my favorite teacher!"

4. Don't raise your hand for every question, but jump in when it's crickets out there, so you're the hero helping the teacher out.

5. Show up early (unlike me on my first day—save the drama for outside the classroom, yuh). Staying after class is so cliché, girl.

6. Support your classmates on their work—it's a win-win for everyone, girl.

SIX

My Mahalo to the Māhū

[Content warning: contains abuse, violence, suicidal thoughts.]

I'm such a strong believer in having a positive personality that I barely like talking about my feelings. I'm just averse to the idea of pity parties—I don't want everybody to be sad with me, and I hate the trauma porn dump thing. That being said . . . mental health is important to me, for you, for everyone. Even though my life may look perfect online because I live in a pretty place and I'm cute, it's not all glitter and rainbows all the time. I have shit I'm dealing with, too, but I've never even been in therapy, so keep that in mind when you read what I'm about to share, which I'm only doing in case my stories help anyone out there get through some similar tough times.

I was officially diagnosed with ADHD when I was in fifth

grade. When you're that young, you don't know what mental health is, you don't know what ADHD is, you don't even know how to spell ADHD. I've been told from an early age that I had issues keeping still, like when I would take a test, even though I was a smart kid. I got very physical a lot. I hate admitting this, but whenever I got frustrated, I'd hit or push my friends and pull their hair. For a little while in elementary school, the Bretman Rock brand was "a very bright but annoying bully, who can't keep still," according to my teachers. Doctors offered me pills and therapy, but the word *therapy* really scared me, because the first time I ever heard it, it was through that court therapist during my parents' separation. She hadn't really acted like a therapist, more like an acting coach, making me remember dates and awful things that happened between my mom and dad. No fucking thank you.

I didn't take the ADHD diagnosis seriously, or see it as something that would hold me back. Even when I got diagnosed with a lazy eye in third grade, I didn't take it seriously. I was not about to pull up to school with a cringey eye patch, looking like an ugly-ass pirate. Yes, she had the lazy eye and was the ADHD girl. She had it all.

Bitch, I still have a lazy eye and can't see out of that eye all that well. And if I'm on an airplane or in a meeting, I still jump out of my skin just having to sit still for so long. I know how people usually act on planes, but I can't lie to you, there are times when all I want to do is push-ups and jumping jacks and hundred-meter dashes in the aisle. And do not seat me next to the fire exit. Like, girl, do not seat anybody with ADHD next to a fire exit. Because that whole five-hour flight, I'll be sweating profusely trying to stop myself from opening it. My brain desperately wants to open it. Just let me touch it. Once! If you tell me not to touch things that makes me want to touch things more.

My extra energy and fidgeting has usually manifested physically but I definitely do feel a mental challenge with the ADHD as well. I have had a lot of episodes where I'd get into arguments and want to hurt myself. I never want to get to a point where I'm super frustrated, you know? But because it wasn't part of my family's culture to really talk about these things, I learned to mask my ADHD and my anxieties and anger. And maybe that's not good either, but thinking about my mental health drains me so much. It's just something that I'm not used to talking about, I guess. I don't even like talking about it much now—it changes my mood drastically for the worse. Even though I have such an elephant brain and I remember so much, my brain is also so good at deleting memories it doesn't want to remember. When I'm trying to speak about mental health, my brain doesn't want to remember the traumas, but, bitch, now that I'm older, I'm trying to learn how to process.

I loved school, and I had an incredible group of friends, but the same dumbass group of boys at school used to bully me, pointing out every day that I was a FOB ("Fresh Off the Boat") and gay, as if nobody knew the gay part. The same ones who catcalled and bullied me would be asking me to suck their dicks in the bathroom as a joke later . . . but was it a joke? Do the math.

I started to dress more feminine as I got older and braver in middle school, like wearing leggings. I'll never forget the day I dared to wear blue fucking pants to school. I had to walk by the younger kids, and they shouted out, "Those pants are ugly!" "Those pants are for girls!" Even the security guard let out the biggest chuckle as I walked by. Little kids are cruel, and I can't believe I let them ruin my day.

But my main bullies were always the football boys. In eighth grade, I started making and wearing haku flower crowns, and no one could dress-code me because they are part of Hawaiian culture. I would rip up my auntie's fake flower vases and hot-glue flowers on my cousin's chicken wire. The best part about it was that you could keep adding flowers onto them, so my hakus just kept getting bigger and bigger and bigger.

The football players all had woodshop, and I had to pass by that class every morning. And of course when I'd walk by in my crown, they'd yell "Faggot!" and "Māhū!" The first time I was ever called māhū was in elementary school, when I refused to play tag with the boys at recess because I'd rather play with the girls. They all called me "māhū" and laughed. I didn't know the word, but seeing how everybody reacted, I realized it was meant to be mean.

For the longest time I thought that *māhū* was just the Hawaiian word for faggot. I didn't learn the true meaning of the word until I had Ms. T during my junior year of high school. Turns out it's a Polynesian word, and it's not even derogatory! Back in the olden days, māhū were accepted as a "third gender," and had really cool spiritual and social roles. Māhū were teachers, priests, and healers. Parents would even ask them to name their children. I mean, who does that? It's funny because there's also a third gender celebrated in Filipino culture, too, babaylan. Babaylans were traditionally shamans and healers and could be male, female, or trans. It's kind of a shame that I didn't know that *māhū* and *babaylan* were both such beautiful words and spiritual roles until later in life. It made no sense for the kids to call me "māhū" in a negative way. Those boys probably didn't even know that their own ancestors included māhūs, or that they had been complimenting me the whole time.

Over time I earned some street cred, and people stopped calling me māhū, or at least not to my face. But I never forgot the word or its powerful symbolism after Ms. T taught us about it. In fact, later down the road, after I became successful and created my makeup palette for Morphe, I named one of the golden highlighter shades Māhū.

But back in my school days, I didn't have the knowledge or confidence to say "Look up to me, bitch. I am māhū." The abuse, especially over being gay, was a lot to deal with, and it hurt me a lot. Being Asian and an immigrant, my mom also didn't understand that I was feeling anxious or that I had ADHD—she thought I was just being dramatic. People her age, who grew up in different times and places, also don't really believe in mental health issues, since when they were growing up, the attitude was usually "Just suck it up, you're fine."

I'm so sensitive about talking about mental health. I will talk about it, but I don't like to shove it down people's throats. But the honest vulnerable truth is that when I was growing up, I was suicidal—there were times when I wanted to vanish. Now I realize that while my family was largely so accepting of my queerness, the ones who didn't accept me did still get to me. The more I think about it, the more I remember little instances of non-acceptance that stick out to me now. Like when I was still living in the Philippines, I remember saying something mean to my sister, Princess, and then my cousin saying, "You're only teasing her because you're gay."

I was really hurt, and I specifically remember my dad, my hero, hearing about it later and not coming to my defense that time, the way he had when my uncle called me "baklâ." I felt defeated.

I'm a Leo, and my dad's a Leo. He fucking knew damn well that our blood type is pride. I felt so ashamed of being called gay, and so angry that my dad hadn't stuck up for me, that I stood outside my house in the burning hot sun for two hours, refusing to come inside, hoping . . . to die. I was so fucking thirsty and dehydrated. When I finally went inside the house, I realized nobody had been paying attention to me. So I needed to be more dramatic. I decided to hide under a big heavy comforter on a bed and try suffocating myself. Nobody knew I was in there—nobody even knew I was hurting so badly—and I eventually passed out from the heat and dehydration. By the time they finally found me the following dawn, my eyes were rolled back, my lips were pale, and I was unresponsive. My mom kept shaking me and was screaming so loud the whole village descended on my house. I finally snapped to, and my mom couldn't stop crying.

When the bullying at school and home got so bad in Hawaii in grade school, I tried to suffocate myself with a blanket again in my bed before school. I told myself, "Bret, don't breathe." I remember hearing my grandma watching *Wheel of Fortune* in the other room before I passed out. I wasn't found until after school by my auntie. But you know what's so wild? After that second attempt, something in me snapped. I was tired of feeling that way, so I toughened up my skin. I also realized I couldn't shove all the abuse down and not deal with it. Something I was taught all the way back in the Philippines was to have humility and compassion. Even though those football boys were punk-ass bitches, I tried to put myself in their not-cute shoes. And here's what clicked in my head: The bottom line is that the biggest insecurity for a lot of straight cis boys (not all, don't @ me) is constantly questioning their own masculinity. In school, I

78

don't think they actually disliked me because I was gay; it was because I was actually more confident and more masculine (and also more athletically gifted) than a lot of them. Physical and mental strength has nothing to do with gender. Just because I'm gay doesn't make me weaker. And that made them vulnerable. So they acted out toward me.

After that realization, I started not giving a shit about what they thought about me. I understood that they were just projecting. Maybe they wanted to be more like me, maybe they wanted me and couldn't deal. Who knows. It could have been a million different reasons for any of them. After this I went back to school, and no one ever would have guessed that I'd been suicidal. The realizations kicked me into gear. This is going to sound dramatic, but this was the point when I started taking school even more seriously, pushing myself to be the best in everything I did. I know for a lot of people, recovery doesn't happen like this, almost overnight, and that real outside help is needed. I just had no other choice at the time but to just push forward, forgive, and give empathy to who I could, including myself.

The boys at school no longer mattered to me. But my brother, J.R., still mattered—and still matters. I used to think my brother had no feelings or soul, but I love my brother now. In the last few years, because of COVID and other illnesses, I've lost so many family members. It's just so hard to hate any of my family members, to hold grudges, at this point, or ever, really. And both of us have changed, and grown up since then.

I tried to have compassion and perspective about J.R.'s bullying and understand where he was coming from. I realized he was projecting his anger onto me. He and my dad were very close when he was growing up, though my dad was going through a rough period then. But after I was born, suddenly I was my dad's angel. I think J.R. was very jealous about that, and that resentment stuck with him as we both got older, even after we'd left our dad behind. He continued to be a very, very angry person until his own kids were born. Now, it's so weird: my brother is suddenly totally for the gays. He's finally making a huge effort to learn about the LGBTQ+ community. In fact, he just asked me the other day what all the letters stand for. He comes to me now to help educate him on the "lesbian, gay, bi, trans, queer."

The other day J.R. asked me why I corrected him all the time on Keiffer's pronouns. "He's still a *he*," he said.

"Well, J.R., you will always see her as Keiffer. And I will always see her as Keiffer as well. But that's her pronoun now. You have to try, at least. And she appreciates that."

I was so glad he even asked about it. Small stuff like that is actually huge for him. My brother's journey has been beautiful to me because when I was a boy, I never could have fathomed J.R. asking me anything about being gay.

Now that we're adults, I've spoken to my brother about his bullying, but I don't think he knows how to apologize. However, he's been around in my life more than ever lately. His love language, and maybe his apology for how he treated me growing up, have become acts and services. He does things for me now, like mowing my yard and putting the flooring down in my gazebo. I still love him, flaws and all—I mean, I'm full of flaws as well.

How am I still here and still so positive every day? I had to teach myself resilience as a little kid. Something I was always telling myself as I was getting bullied for not knowing English, for being an immigrant, for being new to America, for being gay, for messing up, or for no reason at all, was, "I have to make this work." I knew there was so much more I still had to do with my life—that my friends, my teachers, and my family believed in me. I remembered how grateful I was to be here, and that I had so much I looked forward to. That resilience and empathy I developed as a kid shaped me into who I am. I truly believe that anyone is capable of learning, changing, and evolving. I mean, if J.R. can do it, anyone can. I forgive J.R. And that's all that matters now.

How to Deal with Bullies

Buddy up

> Surround yourself with your allies so you never feel alone. If I wasn't defending myself, my besties Bri, Britney, Khrizza, and Laura got my motherfucking back, you know what I mean?

Don't have a big reaction

> They want you to cry or have a big reaction, but not showing that you care takes away their power. Remember, they're bullying you because they're feeling fragile about something.

Disarm the bully with humor

> I swear that's how I did it. If you thought you're funny, I'm a motherfucking clown. If you think you're smart, I'm a fucking genius—like, girl, don't play with me. Keep 'em laughing, and next thing you know, they could be your friend. And no one wants to make fun of the funny kid.

Prepare the perfect comeback

> This doesn't mean insult the bully back, because that's reacting. Besides, "An eye for an eye makes the whole world blind," as Gandhi is supposed to have said. So if the bully

is immune to your jokes and charm, say something sassy instead, like "I've been called far worse by my grandma," or better yet, "This is so boring, darling. I'm moving on."

Walk away

Question their shit, but also don't give them the satisfaction of engaging for too long.

Tell an adult

That's not being a narc, that's being smart.

Hurt people hurt people

Sometimes a bully isn't really putting you down per se—they're more so directing some of the anger they feel toward themselves onto someone else. I know it's hard—but having compassion for your bully might make things hurt less.

SEVEN

I Can Be Whatevah

I've always been (99.9 percent) comfortable with my sexuality. I love being gay. Being a little different has never been an issue, and I don't want to be like everybody else. (Except I do still eat bananas with a fork, because I get uncomfortable when people watch me eat a banana, and not just because I'm gay.) But sexuality and gender are two separate things, and I cannot and will not lie—it took a little longer for me to be brave enough to express my feminine side openly.

My very first experience with gender fluidity was while I was watching this mermaid show in the Philippines. There's just something about queer kids and mermaids that makes sense. Maybe because they don't have genitalia, so we don't know if they're a boy or a girl. We don't know what's under that tail. This mermaid also had really big lips, and I always had big lips, too. That lip representation meant a lot. I was all, "I'm mermaid as fuck."

Most mermaids wish for legs; this mermaid
wishes for chicken wings.

I think I started to come into more of my femininity in elementary school, when my sister and I started to wear the same size clothing. I found myself drawn to her crop tops with a magnetism stronger than the gravitational pull of the earth. It also helped a lot that I lived with a lot of older girl cousins, and they were always bored. They dressed up Keiffer, Colin, and me in their clothes and made us compete against each other for the house pageant crown (you can take a girl out of the Philippines, but we'll still figure out a way to have a pageant). We'd have a bikini contest and a Q&A, but we were too broke for evening gowns, so they held a nightgown portion (it was def more casual wear, girl) instead. That was the first time I put on a bikini and was like, Hmmm, I like this.

The girls would only give us five minutes to put on our makeup between events. I first learned how to put on makeup watching my teenage cousin Jorlie. She gave me her expired, half-used products but I didn't care. Feeling rushed, like, Oh god, I need more time than this, I'd quickly apply lipstick and sprinkle baby powder all over my face until I looked white as fuck (thanks, colorism) and then start performing for the cousins. I remember prancing around as the girls took photos of us, and looking over at Ms. K and Colin, who were clearly not taking these home pageants as seriously as I was. Bitch, when I tell you I was so poised, I gave it my all, and I won. Every time. The prize for second runner-up was $1, first runner-up $2, and the winner received $3 and a mac and cheese bowl, a highly coveted snack in our house. I don't even know why the fuk I was so excited to win that, bitch—I'm lactose intolerant. When my mom and aunties got home, I would show them our pageant pictures proudly. There was no negativity around the pageants other than Colin crying because he got last place. Even my uncles would laugh about them.

"You guys look so pretty!" they all raved. "Who won?"

I mean, me, duh. There's a huge difference between dressing up in women's clothing for yourself, in the safety of your own home with people who know you and love you, and asking the rest of the world to accept you. But by the time the rest of the world has accepted, you realize that the most important people who really need to accept you are just the people you love. I'm so grateful for the space those pageants gave me to explore and show myself and my family my feminine side, and we still talk about those competitions to this day. Those pageants brought our family together in the States, just like how pageants used to bring us together back in the Philippines. Anyway, where was I? Oh yes. I know that expressing your feminine side when you're born a guy is easier said than done. Even for me, going out into the world wearing women's clothing started with bébé steps. In fifth grade I wore a two-piece bikini in another play, but for the longest time after that, I buried the estrogen-infused part of myself in public, especially with all the bullying. As I got older and more and more experimental with my look—one time I wore a flower crown, blue lipstick, and pink shorts to school—I had to defend myself. Kids would tease, "Are you trying to be a girl?" and "Hey Bret, are you wearing lipstick?"

"What do you think?" I clapped back. "Have you ever seen anyone with actually blue lips?"

I don't know if I'd call it going back into the closet exactly, but I had a girlfriend in seventh grade named Jasmine, even though I was gay as fuck and everybody knew it. Everybody was still like, How will you know you don't like girls if you never tried it? Oh my God, this is going to sound so problematic, but Jasmine was just very tomboyish. She reminded me of my girl cartoon crushes, like Kim Possible. She was not afraid to say what was on her mind, and she had masculine energy. I think if you met her today, you'd be like, Bitch, how are you not a lesbian?

But I could not kiss Jasmine. We broke up after a month, and that was that. I was like, Well, tried it, and now I know I don't like it, okay? After my girlfriend (bitch, saying "my girlfriend" makes me giggle), I went *hella* fucking gay. Like *super* fucking gay. I started being even more bold about showing off my feminine side in public.

The first time I realized I was pretty was in eighth grade. Mind you, I was still ugly at the time. But one day before I left for school, I decided to do my eyebrows (I was putting on the $1 Jordana eyebrow powder), and I looked in the mirror in my cousin's room and said out loud to myself, "You are model as fuck. You are so beautiful. I have makeup on today, and I will take your man." It was a little bit delusional, but I believed what I was saying. I've never felt ugly since then.

I think the reason why I think I'm beautiful specifically is because I don't think anybody else looks like me. The most beautiful people in this world are the most different looking or the ones who embody every single feature and every single flaw, every single imperfection that they have, like my two different eyelids that I inherited from my grandparents. That's what beauty is to me. After spending so much time in the industry, I have yet to see a bitch look like me. I have yet to see another magazine cover that features a model like me before me. My uniqueness and my features and how I embody masculine and feminine energy. I'm unique as fuck.

Dressing more femme was actually easier than it needed to be. Fortunately, I lived in a house full of women, and because we were tight on money, I didn't have many other choices beyond women's hand-me-down jeans. To even take the fucking bus to the mall and window shop was a privilege. To be honest, if my mom weren't working two jobs with no days off, I'm sure she would've bought me a dress in a heartbeat, after she beat the owner down first to get a bargain. Sometimes I'd go to school and this kid Bill (Not Billy or Willy or William, a little fucking kid named Bill) would be like, "Those are your sister's pants!" "¿Cómo se dice?" I clapped back. What do you want me to say to that, Bill? How about you say instead, "Love those jeans, your sister has great fashion sense."

It's so funny because in hindsight, I was a cute-ass trendsetter. I wore skinny jeans before fucking Justin Bieber wore skinny jeans. Boys would be like, "Can you even breathe?"

"Bitch, my fucking nose is up here, bitch," I responded coolly. "My nose is not on my leg. What do you mean, can I fucking breathe? Yes, I can."

And tell me why after Justin Bieber wore skinny jeans, the next school year, oh my God, *all* these boys were wearing skinny jeans. Another time I knew I was a trendsetter in my school was when I started wearing Toms shoes. (Remember how they brainwashed a whole society to buy them because they swore they were going to donate one pair of shoes for every shoe bought? Anyways . . .) I thought the slippers were cute and made me look like a ballerina. I could do a pointe in those. But when I started wearing them, all I heard was, "Those are girls' sandals!"

"Bitch, if you look at the label, it says women's size 10, men's 8. Why the fuck would they put the men's size in there if it was just for women?"

I had this conversation with so many boys, over and over again. "When you look at your fucking Converse, look at the bottom of your fucking shoes. It shows the men's and the women's sizes. Look at your Vans. Tell me why you and your girlfriend have matching Vans, bitch. And why do we all have the same Jan-Sport bags? Bitch, clothing is not gender. And I look cute. Fuck you, Cody."

But I must have had some influence on them, because the next year, the boys all got Toms in every color of the rainbow, every print, after this kid called Tony started wearing them. Tony got to walk around in his motherfucking red Toms, and not one word was said to him? I guess because he was Samoan and big and tough and on the football team. Now because Tony was

89

wearing them after football practice, the whole fucking football team had Toms.

Eventually the teasing stopped because people figured out that I was going to wear whatever I wanted and do whatever I wanted to do, and if they had something cute to say to me, I had something cuter to say back. I'd earned my street cred by being bold and staying true to me.

The first time I ever wore makeup to school, though, was such a fail. I hadn't worn makeup out in public since my grandma put blush on my cheeks before church in the Philippines, and then the one time I took my mom's makeup bag and put baby powder all over my face (remember, it would take me a while to embrace my brown skin). I looked white as fuck. I just started putting mascara on, and then I broke her little eyeliner pencil drawing my eyebrows in. I walked around my house the rest of the day like that, waiting for my mom to come home. When she did, she was like, "Oh, you're so pretty." My grandma was the only hater, though, because I got baby powder all over our room that she was trying to clean. She didn't hate on the makeup though, because she knows I woulda shot back that her boobs were on the ground.

Flash forward to the start of eighth grade. I was watching *America's Best Dance Crew,* and a dancer had that slit brow look. I wanted it, too, so I snuck my mom's tweezers and plucked so much that I was left only with a naked strip of painful red bumps. In a panic, I used her mascara brush to paint in my brow before going to school. But it was really humid, and the mascara melted all down my face. My teacher called my mom to rat on me that I wore makeup to school, and I was so scared that I'd get in trouble with her later. Instead, when I got home, my mom said, "Can you

90

translate what your teacher said? Because I don't understand why she called." This was the most iconic thing she could have said to me—I knew she understood what my teacher had said, but my mom didn't see why it was an issue, and she didn't give a shit if I wore makeup in public.

I continued experimenting at home with these tinted lip balms called Baby Lips from Maybelline, the first makeup products I bought with my own money (money I earned myself with all my hustles, yuh). I remember I spent exactly $63 at Long's Drugs on makeup, where I also got my first primer and lip glosses. Just a sheer tint of red gloss on me did so much for my self-esteem. I got good at doing makeup through trial and error. I watched tutorials and practiced on my cousins and on my friends every day, on weekends, too, and when you're doing something that much, it's kind of hard not to get good at it. I put in my ten thousand hours to become an expert. Their compliments encouraged me to keep going and explore makeup even more. I could walk around that whole house with purple eyeshadow and freckles on and a green lip and no one would ask me questions. It was an amazing freedom that I had. I got so good that girls started asking me to cover up their hickeys, like I mentioned earlier. I feel like people look at makeup as just makeup, but I see it as so much more than that. I see makeup as an art form. I see makeup as me. I see makeup the same way that a jock sees a football and it makes him feel happy, or like when a singer sees a mic and feels powerful. I see makeup as possibility.

Vanity became sacred to me; vanity became my passion. I imagine vanity as fire. Fire is a triangle: to create fire you need three ingredients, earth, fuel, and wind. And to ignite a fire with vanity, you need hair, makeup, and fashion. All three of these ingredients are vital to me. Vanity is power. When I am in my makeup, and my hair is done, and I have a cute outfit on, I feel powerful. There's literally no other word to describe it. When I was a kid, I'd watch all these superhero shows, especially Filipino ones—we had one called Lastik Man who I loved because his superpower was being super stretchy. I loved them because they're like one thing in the daytime and then they transform when they have to save lives, you know, be the superhero. And I think there's a type of . . . not exactly gender expression, but something that I wanted in watching these shows growing up, in terms of having the power to go beyond the boundaries of your own body, beyond what people expect you to look like or do. I start as Clark Kent, and then I blossom into Superman when I'm in a full face of makeup, in the right fit, hair fixed just right.

It still took me until sophomore year of high school to show up to school with a full face of makeup on. I'm talking my whole face, contoured, foundation on, reconstructed, highlighted to the gods. I just woke up one day and was like, I'm going for it. I wish I had a more dramatic story like, Oh my God, some kid took a makeup wipe and smeared off my makeup in third period. But by that point, after years of me pushing gender norms, nobody cared. My eye shadow was always motherfucking poppin', but nobody motherfucking ever said anything. Not that I wanted to get bullied, but at least some bad press, come on. I don't know if people were talking shit behind my back, but even my teachers were like, "Oh, you look so pretty." The only thing that sucked was being a teacher's assistant for Mr. Nagamina for PE. Don't get me wrong, I love being athletic and sporty, but just not when I've worked hard to put on a full face of makeup. Mr. Nagamina was the type of bitch who'd just be like, "All right, class, Bretman's

92

going to show us an example of how to run the half-mile relays." Bitch, I just beat my face. Imagine being late to school because you were perfecting your eyebrows and then it melts off in PE in first period. But if anything, at least my daily lewks helped kick my hickey cover-up business up to a whole new level.

After a while I started to do my friends' and cousins' makeup, too, and I just loved witnessing their transformations and seeing their confidence blossom. After I showed them their final faces, they turned into totally different people—I mean, not just from the outside, you could see their light shine from within as well.

People are always asking me, What is the best primer? The best primer is not something you can buy on Amazon, bitch. You can't use my code for 10 percent off. The best primer, the best thing to start with, is your own self-fucking-confidence, and an understanding of who you are. Because if you build your makeup over your insecurities, you're just going to be a pretty, insecure person.

I went to a spiritual healer recently and asked so many questions about my past lives. I told her I felt like I've been gay in all of my lives.

"Yeah," she confirmed. "In all of your lives, you've always been the third gender. In your past lives, though, your throat chakra was stuck, you were never allowed to be loud, you were never allowed to be who you were. Now, in this lifetime, you've been reincarnated to become who you're supposed to be. That's why you're a star. Your ancestors are jumping up and down with joy. You are their wildest dream."

That was so life-confirming for me—I needed this verbal affirmation of who the fuck I was and what I was meant to put out in this world and what I really wanted to do. Also, I've always joked around that if I was ever brought back and given the choice to be straight or gay, I would definitely come back gay. I wouldn't even think twice about it. If anything, I'd be a gay woman coming back to try something different, but I'd definitely still be gay. So this reading from the healer was validating, to know that I've been queer in all my past lives.

If I've felt 99 percent before, today I finally feel comfortable being 1,000 percent me, a perfect blend of masculine and feminine. I don't get upset if you call me "he" when you see me working out, or "she" when I look like a goddess. Call me either, just don't be mean. I know I'm not always perfect—I still have days when my hair looks like pubes.

I don't think anyone is 100 percent one or the other gender, either only gay or straight—everybody is in between. I hate all the labels personally—like I wouldn't call myself nonbinary, but I love that I have precedent in traditions like māhū and babaylan. I know what makes me feel confident, like, I like having muscles and being dirty, and I will also be Miley Cyrus for Halloween. (Bitch, I only got second place for best costume that year, though.) I shop in the girl and boy sections. I'll do cardio with a full face of makeup. I embody both energies.

The moral of the story is, once you get comfortable in your own skin, both your day-to-day skin and figuring out what makes you feel like a superhero, no one can bring you down. You can do anything when you're pretty and handsome at the same time.

Why I Love Plants

Plants don't have a gender; most are hermaphrodites. Maybe that's why I connect with them so spiritually. Before I had real plants in my house, I had fake ones. But I could not feel that sense of aliveness, so they were not filling this need for energy in me. During the early part of the pandemic I was bored, and got obsessed with buying plants. I don't talk to them—I perform for them and play them their favorite song, a play on *Fantasia* called "Plantasia." I swear my plants dance when they hear it.

These are my favorites:

Dried Herbs

My witchy grandma Lilang in the Philippines was an herbalist, so she always had a lot of dried plants around for her potions, mostly guava leaves and other herbs. There's so much healing in plants, my grandma used to say, whether you're using them for medicine or just taking care of them yourself.

Birds of Paradise

These are the flowers I used to cut and put on my grandpa's grave. (And I have a tattoo of them.)

Philodendron joepii

Out of all the categories of plants (succulents, cacti, and so on), philodendron are my favorite because there are so many types of them, five hundred species around the world. Leos like to collect things so I have a lot of choices

here but *Philodendron joepii* is one of the rarest philodendron species in the world and I own one. I transformed my
pit bull Ele's dog house into a sanctuary for my rare plants.
I'm a rare plant collector now, I would say. The best
part about being rich is that I can have a rare plant
collection.

Dealing with Insecurity

Sometimes you just don't feel like that bitch. Other people's opinions can get in, even if your intention going into something is *I'm just doing me, and I'm happy with it.* If people don't think you deserve something, it shouldn't matter, because like, don't we tell that to ourselves enough already? Like trust—whatever someone says to you, you've probably heard it before.

Make boundaries for yourself, between your work self, your public self, and who you really see yourself as. Like for me, Bretman Rock and Bretman have different fucking problems and issues. You know what I mean? And like when I say I don't give a fuck, it's really just like Bretman is learning to not give a fuck about Bretman Rock's problems. If I'm literally crying in a hotel room by myself and it's like this because of people who've never met me, I'm like, What would Bretman say looking at Bretman Rock right now? Like, girl, you really had a mental breakdown at your motherfucking hotel room because people had something to say about how you—so cringey. You might not be crying in a penthouse, but when you are crying about something, take time to look at what you do have, and what matters more than whatever the fuck someone who doesn't know the real you at all just said to you.

EIGHT

Too Short to Be a Stripper

While my other classmates were busy hooking up with each other, I was busy becoming Bretman Rock. I didn't date anyone the whole time I was in school (my middle-school girlfriend does not count), so I thought I was asexual at some point, because everyone at my school was ugly. I mean, my back cramped up from carrying the only cute genes at my school. Instead of getting STDs, though, I got famous by the time I was fifteen as a content creator.

Everybody always wants to know how I did it. It started with my name. Being named after two wrestlers, Bret "The Hitman" Hart and Dwayne "The Rock" Johnson, has defined my life from the minute I catwalked out of my mom's snatch. Way before I was The Bretman Rock, people were already telling me I had a "star's name." You know, names that just roll off the tongue and have that celeb-y vibe, like Rihanna, Zendaya, or Beyoncé. When people said that, I always wondered, What is a star? The seed was planted very young.

My marquee name plus my bottomless need for attention created the perfect storm. While I was starring as the school's morning presenter on Lima TV, I officially dropped my last name, Sacayanan, and from then on I was forever known as Bretney Spears or Bretman Rock, and I treated myself as if I was genuinely already famous. Walking to high school every morning, I put my headphones on and blasted generic audio of crowds cheering. (I literally googled "concert screaming" and found some good ones from *Hannah Montana* and played that instead of music.)

It was unfortunate that I couldn't find anybody legit screaming my name anymore (like they did in elementary school) as I rolled in, but I also had the headphones on because I had to walk past an intermediate school every morning to get to my high school, and if there's anything about inter-fucking-mediate kids, they're cruel as hell, the meanest motherfuckin' creatures in this world. Girl, you can't scream taunts and "Māhū!" at me if a full concert's worth of people are already screaming in my ear. I'd smirk as I paraded by with my hundred-yard model stare, thinking, Bitch, one day you guys are for real going to be freaking out while I'm walking to school. Also, go google "māhū."

It was small things like that and my confessionals in front of the mirror or the Walmart security cameras, along with continued manifestations of fame (even if this particular one was a combination of being a lil' delusional and not wanting to hear the catcalls and shit from intermediate school kids), that put me on my track to stardom.

The other important piece of the puzzle on my journey to fame and fortune was the invention of camera phones (bitch, I couldn't just go to Walmart every time I wanted to be recorded doing something). The first time I saw that my mom's phone had a camera, I literally started crying, "Oh my God, this is all I ever wanted!" I'm not exaggerating. Any time I saw a lens, the idea of being on-screen became my whole world, even if it was just a few pixels.

There was one major hitch: my mom wouldn't get me my own phone for the longest fucking time. She'd given me a phone to call her when I was a toddler in the Philippines, but after I came to America, she didn't allow us to have phones because my cousins also didn't have phones. Girl, that was a bullshit excuse. The bitch just didn't want to buy me a phone (not me calling my Scorpio mom a bitch . . .).

Other kids got phones (and boyfriends) in sixth and seventh grade. They were keeping up with the world. Not this bitch. I only got an iPod. I could communicate with people if I had an internet connection, obviously. There were plenty of times back then when my friends would be planning fun activities, and I'd have to run all the way to McDonald's for Wi-Fi to be on the group chat. If we were going to the mall, I'd have to run to the McDonald's next to the bus stop just to tell them I was on the way. Hop on the bus, get to the mall, find the nearest Wi-Fi hotspot and text, "Where are y'all at? I'm here." It was a pain in my phat ass.

My mom had one of those burner phones that didn't even come with a T-Mobile or AT&T plan. It only had like a five-gigabyte memory but, drumroll please, it did have that phone camera. I used to steal her phone and make two-minute videos doing the most embarrassing shit on it, making faces, screaming, which was all that it could handle. When she noticed, she started yelling, "I can't even save any numbers because you keep recording these dumb videos!" But I still didn't get my own phone (with a camera) until like freshman year, if you can imagine.

Shortly after, in 2012, and at the tender age of twelve, I posted my very first video masterpiece on Facebook: reading a dirty Valentine's poem I found on Tumblr. I read it to my friends and they were cracking up. Before that my online presence was just me posting typical text posts on Facebook, like how I'd farted two times in class and blamed it on someone else. (That only got three likes.) My post saying, "Rest in peace Whitney Houston even though I have no idea who you are" got a pathetic twenty-one likes. But the video of me reading that poem got fifty fucking likes, which was a huge milestone for me. I was over the moon that anyone cared.

One day I want to hunt each of those fifty people down and give them a gift, because they were the reason I kept going with my videos. When I look back at my old videos, it was mostly just my friends commenting and hyping me up. I was just so blessed with great friends—they kept pushing me to keep making videos. They were such free souls, and I loved making them crack up. It's so fucking embarrassing, but even before my videos, I'd always do skits and poems in front of them, like:

You're my light and my dark
And you make me hard
Your booty is full of cooties
And I want to get in your coochie.

101

Without them, I don't think I would ever have truly found Bretman Rock.

My friends would always compare me to an early YouTube creator named Ryan Higa, one of the first creators from Hawaii to make it viral. We all looked up to him, because he was Asian and from Hawaii. I was obsessed with him and skipped school once to go to his meet-and-greet at a local mall.

"Don't you want to be like Ryan Higa?" they asked me. Bitch, I did. Eventually I moved my videos to YouTube, but it would take a little trial and error to get to Ryan Higa's level. We never ended up collaborating but I did finally get to meet him at a gaming event. He didn't know who I was and was like, "Are you from Hawaii?" So that was kind of a buzzkill.

My first YouTube videos were basic af, like eating a roach from the Philippines when I visited there and doing leg wind-mills, but I soon realized people enjoyed it when I was just twerk-ing and cursing and being 100 percent myself on social media. Within two years, I was getting fifty thousand views per video on Instagram and Snapchat. People were eating my shit up, and I just kept finding more things that I enjoyed doing on camera. The possibilities felt endless.

As my audience grew, I got unofficially inducted into the micro influencers club, you know, where they were all doing shout-out-for-shout-outs to swap or add followers. At this point, all I wanted—all *we* wanted—was fame. Those early days were such a different time to be an influencer. It genuinely took a lot of time and effort to be famous back then, so you really had to want it, and then you might need a little luck. Nowadays you can get a million followers overnight because of algorithms. The new influencers have help from the apps. Back then you got your fame from word of mouth and really earned it. We were all just making videos left and right, posting without even thinking. This was an ignorant, experimental era of my career and of my life. Sometimes I think about things I would do or say when I was younger and I'm mortified. But the internet never forgets. When I got to about ten thousand followers, my numbers plateaued for a hot minute. Then, one fateful afternoon, I was trying to record myself dancing dramatically to Beyoncé's "Smack It in the Air" in our living room, and had asked my sister, Princess, to wait before crossing in front of me to get through to the other side of the room. But the bitch walked through my shot anyway, carrying her stupid-ass red Solo Cup, ruining my best take yet—so I reflexively smacked the back of her ponytail super hard. The way her hair went, girl, and the way I snarked, *"Are you fucking serious?"*—well, that shit went viral, periodt.

That was a watershed moment—I went from 10,000 followers to 2.5 million almost overnight, and the rest is herstory. I never looked back.

The second video that took me to the next level was my makeup tutorial, a "How to Contour" video. I'd made a bold announcement on Instagram that I was going to be doing more makeup content— I'd been wearing makeup at home and at school but never publicly in videos at this point. I mean, men have worn makeup since the beginning of time—Scott Barnes, Dimitri James, and Kevyn Aucoin, to name a few—but it was sort of unheard of for a younger, openly gay boy to teach people how to wear makeup.

It was like the spirit of Beyoncé possessed me, and my life's purpose had become clear. It wasn't being a stripper anymore. (My backup plan in case acting or being a content creator didn't work out—I mean there's a good reason I had a stripper pole in my bedroom, duh.) I dropped the contouring video on Instagram as sixteen separate videos, uploaded every five minutes (at the time, Instagram didn't have the slides), after which someone compressed it all into one video, which they then uploaded onto Facebook. That video solidified me in the makeup industry and it's what made Bretman Rock, Bretman Rock. At the time I was recording and posting, I didn't think I was doing anything revolutionary (it makes me so happy to see so many boys in makeup now), until the likes started rolling in, and my mom said I looked "cute." She never said I looked cute. Beauty, which had become a huge part of my life, truly became an inextricable part of who I am. What made me famous was being 100 percent me—vanity and beauty and makeup.

It was total chaos after that video went viral. I started getting hundreds of thousands of followers every hour, the DMs were pouring in. I had unlocked a lot of videos that had been set to private, so that by the time they came to my pages there was so much content there. I remember being glued to my new phone and I kept refreshing, going OMG OMG OMG. From that moment on, my phone would never be off again, unless I went on vacation. But back then I was new to all of it—to say I was very excited about all the attention is the understatement of the century.

After that, it was so easy to go viral over and over again. I mean, the other day I backed up too fast while I was dancing to a Bruno Mars song, and I hit my ass on the door, and it went viral on TikTok, five million views. Who the fuk knows why? This shit comes so fucking natural to me now, especially after years of entertaining my family and friends. The hardest part of my job now is staying relevant and creative without losing my soul or my mind—I don't know exactly why some of my content works the way it works, but all I know is that I'd rather be relevant for falling on my ass than weird drama or bad shit.

Just like Ryan Higa before me, I became a local celebrity—like I did a radio interview with two straight men, and I remember them saying, Do you realize your number of followers is double the population of Hawaii? At the time the population was around 2 million, and I had like 3.7 million followers. "Oh my gosh, I could overthrow Hawaii," I joked as cutely but as seriously as possible. But really, that many people was hard to fathom.

Local TV news wanted in on the Bretman Rock action, too. At the time I didn't have a manager, so a reporter (now anchor, congrats on your promotion) named Brenton Awa from KITV Island News emailed me directly, but wanted to talk to me in the middle of third period. I was like, Bitch, what the fuck. But yeah, he came to my school, and no one gave a fuck (although until he showed up, I didn't know Mr. Brenton was that cute). People already knew me as Mr. Aloha, Mr. Popular, Mr. Extra, at school, so to be honest, you can't be famous twice. It'd be like double jeopardy. The only ones who really cared about these interviews were my friends' moms. They'd always trusted me with their daughters because I wasn't going to be the one smoking a joint in the bathroom with them during third period, I was going to be on the news, yuh. I wasn't a troublemaker—if anything, their daughters were the bad example. They'd always say, "You made me want to have a gay son," which makes me really proud to hear because I know not every family is as accepting as mine. But because of that local news interview the whole island knew who I was, and I've felt nothing but love and support ever since. Hawaii is where Bretman Rock the influencer was born, bred, and nurtured.

A couple of weeks after the TV interview, I got recognized while at the movies by a girl named Chelsea from Oahu (we still DM to this day). After Chelsea, fans popping up to say hi just kept happening so I thought, Is it time to meet people? It seems like it's what the people want. So I set up a meet-and-greet at the mall by posting a video about it. "I'm going to be in the mall walking around. If you see me say hi, bitch." People showed the fuck up. (I mean, there were also people that were just like at the mall to get Sbarro, but whatever.) I wound up making a whole collage afterward of everybody who showed up and took a picture with me.

My first meet-and-greet in the Philippines, featuring Mom

Good shit was happening at a pace I couldn't keep up with. I never actually realized when it all got to be too much for a single person to handle—I mean, I actually still don't know what is "too much" for Bretman Rock. I knew at some point that I needed help, but I had no idea where to turn. I was still just sixteen years old. I went through two not-great manager situationships—the first was a twenty-year-old who knew less than I did but talked a big game, and the next one didn't get me at all. She called me a "spectacle" to my face (and not in a cute way), and sniffed that I would eventually flop, fade away, and my brand would never live on or amount to anything. Hearing those things from someone who was supposed to lead me in my career hurt and had a lasting impact on how I saw myself. That shit stayed with me longer than I ever imagined or wanted.

So I thank my lucky stars I found my perfect manager, Dru. I knew she was good people when I flew in from Hawaii to LA, and she'd asked me how my flight was. I told her a funny story about how the ninety-year-old man almost died right next to me, and she was dying cackling. She told me that I was a legit comedian. That was the first time somebody called me something other than an influencer. Her vibe wasn't, *Let me milk Bretman for all he's worth, then toss him aside when whatever he's doing becomes so ten minutes ago.* Dru's vibe was, *This kid has what it takes to make it to the top.*

Find you someone who believes in you one million percent. No, infinity percent. Dru didn't look at me as a client or a commodity or just work. She saw the reality in my fantasies, and I was also a part of her dreams, something bigger. Dru and I fell in love. And we will stop at nothing to reach our goals together. Once we became a team, amazing offers came pouring in and we said yes to everything, duh.

Commercials and shows and podcasts and video game collabs started happening. When I was twenty-two my idol Michelle

This was taken on the trip where
Dru said I'm a comedian.

Obama named me a cochair for her "When We All Vote" drive (I was beyond honored), with people like Selena Gomez, Tom Hanks, Liza Koshy, Janelle Monáe, Lin-Manuel Miranda, Steph Curry, Megan Rapinoe, Shonda Rhimes, and Kerry Washington to drive voter registration, education, and turnout in the midterms and future elections to help change the culture around voting and close race and age gaps. I mean, are you fucking kidding me?

Biz peeps really started to trust the idea of Bretman Rock and just allow me to be myself. Brands stopped sending me scripts and started sending me blank pages. Now the messaging was like, Just do whatever you want. The corporations saw the most success when they let me be me. Being able to convince people of this is one of the most powerful things I've done in my career.

Dru and I put in the work using our own formula. Even with my merch, we do our own thing. We don't go to other people—we try to create everything ourselves, because we feel like that's how we can learn the most. And I think it's working. Actually, bitch, I *know* it's working. In 2017 *Time* magazine named me one of its "30 Most Influential Teens." In 2018 *Forbes* put me on their "30 Under 30 Asia—Media, Marketing & Advertising" list. At this point, I've collabed with Klarna, Sephora, Nike, Morphe, ColourPop Cosmetics, Wet n Wild, Curology, Crocs, Ole Henrikson, Dime Optics, and Sims.

I've shattered some wild glass ceilings already. I was the first gay man on the cover of *Playboy* (more on that in a second). I'm an ambassador for Nike, even though I don't even play a mother-fucking sport. I've been included and celebrated and dressed by A-list designers in the fashion industry, not exactly a hotbed of diversity for brown Asian immigrants without inherited wealth. Look what I've already done, just by believing I could, being myself, and fucking around and having fun. This is why I know I can go the distance. It's not even about awards or being on lists in magazines, though those are cute, please keep them coming. It's stuff like this: the other day I was at Brandy Melville—I don't usually shop there, my friend was exchanging her skirt—and I hate waiting for bitches, so I was wandering around and finding cute stuff. When I went up to the cashier to pay for it, the girl ringing me up was like, "Hi, I don't want to be creepy, but can I show you something?" And she pulled out a picture that we had taken together in 2015 at my first meet-and-greet. She had been ten years old then, and now she was a grown-ass eighteen-year-old woman.

Damn, I thought, I've really been at this a while, huh? And I got all teary-eyed, and once again I hate crying because I look ugly when I cry, so I pulled myself together for her, one of my true OGs. But later I couldn't stop thinking about how far I'd come. How people do that all the time to me now, and it still doesn't get old—their pulling out pictures from my first meet-and-greets and telling me how much I've made them happy at terrible times in their lives, how I've influenced the way they see the world, their senses of humor, even the way they talk. And I'm just like wut the fuk and get all emo.

One girl who'd been a fan since the very beginning and had taken a photo with me then was like, "Yo, my mom told me to never delete this picture because she always knew you were going to be so much more. We want to pull it out one day when you come out with your first movie." It's so cool to hear from people who have believed in you for so long, from before you even believed or really knew yourself.

"Bitch," I told this girl, "I really raised you."

"Don't even get me started, I literally take after your personality," she said.

"Yes, you did."

Confidence in yourself is everything. I've always been confident that I had what I needed to reach my very lofty goals. I vividly remember having a big conversation with Dru when we first started working together. I was spitting out all the dreams I had, and we were writing them on a mood/manifesting board.

"I want to go to the Met."

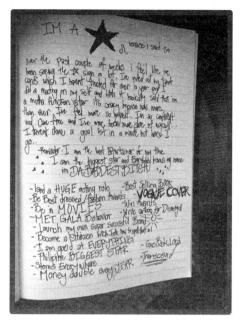

No caption needed, you heard me.

"Okay, then we have to tackle fashion," she said, and put it on the board.

"I want to act."

Duly noted on the board.

"I want to model."

She wrote it down. In pink marker, bitch.

When you think about this list now, you can see how many things we've already ticked off.

"I want to be a sex symbol," I added, not joking at all. Totally serious. "I want to be on the cover of *Playboy* magazine."

A lot of great entertainers are sex symbols. A lot of people that I look up to also exude sex, like Marilyn obvs, and Beyoncé, and Wonder Woman. Prince is the gender-fluid sex icon god that

I want to be. I like to think that I channel Prince when it comes to what I attract, to the way I also exude sex, with nonbinary looks still based in masculinity.

I said it out loud again to manifest it. "I want to be a sex symbol, and I want to be a sexy bunny."

So this is how I know I got the witchy genes from Grandma Lilang. One night last year, I was craving sushi. I was waiting to be seated at a restaurant in Hawaii with my sister, and I was on my phone. I don't even know how I was recognized because I had a hat on, but a woman came up to me, all excited.

"Bretman, can I get a picture with you?"

Obviously, I wasn't going to say no. I never say no.

We had a short conversation, and I thought that was that. Minutes went by when my publicist texted me. "You just met one of my friends, and she works at *Playboy*."

Why the fuck didn't that bitch say so? It just so happened that she was in casting. If I hdan't had a craving for sushi that night, one of the biggest moments of my life might have passed me by.

The lesson is, always listen to your heart and your stomach.

The photo shoot itself was epic. The powers that be decided to put me in a jet-black bunny corset, just like I'd always dreamed, and wearing it did something to me. It was so *Playboy*, and this is so fucking cliché to say, but for once, and I promise the only time, bitch, I'm at a loss for the words to describe the feeling. I'm gonna try anyways. I finally felt like a sex symbol. Like I've always believed that I'm beautiful, but now I finally truly believed it when people told me I was hot, that I felt that other people could see it. It was the first time I just genuinely felt so fully myself, like no one could tell me shit. Every little gay boy deserves to feel like that. Of course, not every gay boy wants to be a sex symbol. Some want to be ice skaters or event planners.

I was so happy when *Playboy* let me pick which of Brian Ziff's photos to use on my cover—I chose the one of me standing like a supermodel, wearing the iconic bunny ears, corset just below my perfect chest, nips out, duh, black tights, black bow tie, white cuffs, and black platform heels. While I was at the shoot, I'm not even gonna lie to you right now, I did not think that the cover would get quite this much attention. I'd seen straight men like Bad Bunny and Bruno Mars on the cover of *Playboy*. (Or at least not out-at-the-time men. Because I get a bisexual vibe from at least one of those bitches. Anyway, we're not here to talk about that.) So I already had in my head they'd done men before, you know, but not wearing a bunny outfit.

I woke up the day it came out, October 1, 2021, knowing that my cover was out and that it was iconic obviously cuz, bitch, I'm iconic, but I didn't know it would be that revolutionary. But that day I became the first openly gay man to be on the *Playboy* cover, the first openly gay man to be by himself on the cover.

I've never been more honored to post anything in my life. I wrote on Instagram: "For *Playboy* to have a male on the cover is a huge deal for the LGBT community, for my brown people community and it's all so surreal. A total 'is this even fucking happening right now?' type of vibe. And I'm so pretty."

The first day my cover came out, it was nothing but positive comments; everyone was so congratulating and warm. I thought I was gonna get some boys hollering at me after they saw it, but that didn't happen. This did not add up. How am I on the cover of *Playboy*, but I have no boys to play with? Howevuh, the response from my community was so great, especially since it debuted at the beginning of Filipino Heritage Month. And my mom was proud. She was like, "Oh my God, my son!" She didn't say "sexy," but the equivalent in English for the word she used is "ferocious." She usually never calls me any word that's even slightly feminine. Even when I'm in a full face of makeup, she's usually always like, "You're so handsome." Ferocious was the most girlie adjective she'd ever used to describe me and it made my heart swell.

But then . . . *dun dun dun* . . . four days later, the big guns started posting about my cover—CNN, *USA Today*, *People* magazine, all of them. They have access to Middle America. Girl, when I tell you it was a landslide, oh my God . . . an avalanche of chaotic-ass comments started rolling in.

Luckily I had already gotten the time to feel myself and collect all of my kudos. Now I started getting a ton of hate from straight middle-aged men, who kept commenting, "Hugh Hefner is rolling over in his grave!" "I'm unsubscribing!" "I'm throwing my copy in the dumpster!" I was like, Baby, last time *Playboy* did print was two years ago. So obviously you don't know anything about *Playboy*. If I've hurt people, that actually bothers me, because that's never my intention to hurt people. But for this, if some straight guy in the suburbs was hurt, I didn't give a fuck. It was comical for me how these images bothered so many people. I was like, "What do you want me to do?" I couldn't help but ask these questions:

Do you want me to unprint them, bitch?

Should I not be gay?

Should I not move history forward?

GTFO.

My favorite was, "*Playboy*, I just lost all respect!" I don't even think *Playboy* gives a single fuck if you respect them. Yes, they've had their fair share of criticism about exploiting women and their body parts. But I did my research, and *Playboy* has also always pushed the envelope and pushed the public discourse forward, not all backassward. In 1965 they featured Martin Luther King Jr., and in 1971 they had Darine Stern as their first African American woman on the cover. In 1991 Caroline Cossey became the first openly transgender woman on the cover of *Playboy*, decades ahead of its time. They've always pushed for abortion rights and legalizing marijuana. People who associate *Playboy* with nothing but women and sex are so narrow-minded.

And last of all, don't be mad if you're like, "Why am I aroused by this?" Embrace it, ho. If this is making you mad, then it's doing what it's supposed to do, which is creating conversations around sexuality. This type of anger is what moves society, it's what makes progress. If you're saying that Bretman Rock doesn't belong here because *Playboy* is for sex, well, sex is for all genders. And if you tell me that *Playboy* is for men, well, gay men are men too. Periodt.

Even though I got a lot of hate online, I know I was able to change so many hearts and minds because I witnessed it with my own two eyes. Back in Hawaii, I took an Uber right after my cover came out and struck up a conversation with the driver. (I'm not one of those pussy-ass bitches who taps "quiet mode.")

"What do you do?" he asked me.

"I'm a model," I answered. Yuh.

"Oh, for who?"

"Actually, I was the first *Playboy* gay cover this month."

"Shut up!" He literally fucking turned around. "I saw that while reading my phone and drinking my coffee this morning! That's you?"

Turns out he had been reading the story when Facebook and Instagram infamously went down for an entire day, so his page was open to it all fucking day long.

"I'm not gonna lie, you're sexy," he said bashfully. "I'm not gay, but you're sexy."

For this big straight Hawaiian man to put his masculinity aside, I could barely even comprehend. It still gives me goose bumps to think about this conversation to this day.

Not long after that happened, I was walking my dogs and my neighbor, he's like this old—oh God, I hate calling people old, but he's a white, silver-haired straight man, and it's relevant to the story, bitch—yelled at me, "Bret, I saw it!"

"What'd you see? My missing chicken, Mazie? Where she at?"

"I saw your *Playboy* cover! Congrats, man. You're so hot!"

Like a sixty-year-old-man calling you hot early in the morning? Cock-a-doodle-do.

Then all these workers who I didn't even fucking see earlier came down from the roof, and just did one of those slow claps like in the movies where one guy starts clapping and then they all join in and everybody cries. It made my day. (Bitch, I said 99.9 percent of this book is true.)

Playboy was one of those things that was supposed to happen in my life. I manifested it, I was meant to have it, and it's empowered me ever since. If that one photo meant anything, it's that I belong in this cultural space. It created the type of change that I could have only imagined when I first started all of this.

Every time I put something out now, I want to top what I've done previously. Since *Playboy*, everything else seems possible—like I've been getting so many visions in my head (and I rarely get visions), but I really feel like this cover is propelling me to something greater, with my higher self and with the universe.

How to Influence the World in 5 Easy Steps

Fuck a niche: I hate having just one niche. I feel like there's a reason why a lot of us experience mental blockage or creativity blockage, because we're like, oh my God, I can only do makeup cuz I'm a beauty girl. Like no, who the fuck said that? You don't have to just be good at one thing online—explore everything that's exciting to you. And there are people like me who are honestly good at everything. So try to be good at everything. Or if you're not good at everything, at least try to be okay at a lot of things.

Be kind to everybody: Don't be afraid to kiss ass sometimes. I feel like the best people I've met are the ones at events and stuff that I just kind of go up to and start talking to. Be kind and talk to everyone, even if they don't look like you. In my earlier days in social media, I was the only fucking bitch at these events who was young, brown, and Asian. And I would like literally just sit there in my corner and wait for someone to come talk to me, but then I realized I had to just start talking to people first. And then you know, I'm talking to the head talent manager at Benefit Cosmetics, and then the next thing you know, I have a fucking commercial with them.

Don't spend too much: Don't spend more than what you make. When you become an influencer, especially when you have your big break, the money, the fame, it'll come fast. But you have to figure out how to keep it going, and how to keep it all sustainable.

Numbers are numbers: They don't define who you are as a creative, as an influencer. I would say our whole fucking careers are very much controlled by numbers, by how many likes we're getting, how many dislikes we're getting, how many comments, how many people are sharing our videos, how much money we're making, what time to post—even times are numbers, you know what I mean? Our whole industry is controlled by numbers. And I think just removing yourself from those numbers is very helpful. Step away from the numbers sometimes. Don't let them define you and your work and your work ethics and where you're headed.

Don't be afraid to log out: Don't forget to step away completely every now and then—log out and drink water!

NINE

My Fat Puss & Butch Body

Girl, the Lord or whatevah higher power you believe in has blessed me with this fat ass. But getting my body in abs-solutely stacked and jacked hourglass shape is about way more than looking good. I've always upkept my mental health and sense of control through physical movement. My dad was my biggest influence when it came to being active. When I was growing up, he let me do whatever I wanted most of the time, but he also made sure I did things that were good for me, too. The other huge influence on me after I came to America was Michelle Obama. President Obama grew up on the other side of my island, and Michelle Obama, girl, that woman really got me moving a lot when I was a little kid. In elementary school I was doing all of Michelle Obama's presidential fitness workouts that she used to do. She was also into growing vegetables and herbs in her garden and whatnot, which I've also gotten into. She actually made a difference. She was a First Lady who actually did something for the youth.

Anyways, from the start, my dad was my biggest fitness supporter. You could probably guess that he was into sports because he named me after wrestlers, but he was a real athlete, too. My dad woke up every morning and did a hundred push-ups.

In my early days, I was a skinny little bitch. And yet, as I've mentioned, before I could even fucking tie my shoes, I used to go jogging with my dad. Before I fell in love with beauty, I fell in love with fitness. Growing up in the Philippines and Hawaii, I was always upside down, running around, and hanging from trees. Except for one stoner period where I was kinda lazy, but we'll get to that. Patience.

The first sport my dad ever put me in was Pony League baseball. We called it "coach pitch" in the old country, because you stood there with a fat bat like a motherfucking idiot while an adult underhanded the ball to you, and then if you hit it, everybody ran around like chickens. I remember being very irritated the whole time because I didn't want to be there, first of all. But also because we didn't really have the best equipment to play. My mom had sent me a baseball mitt she bought from a swap meet, but it was a baseball glove for a six-foot fucking man. Both of my hands could fit in this glove. And we were middle-class compared to other people in town, so every other kid was using a hat to catch the ball, or whatever they could find honestly. Some used winter gloves. I was the cool kid because I had a glove, and cleats. They were soccer cleats, but they were cleats, nonetheless. But two days into the Pony League, I was over it. I realized almost immediately that I

121

wasn't gonna be any good at sports that have too many rules and regulations. I moved on, bitch.

So baseball was a definite ew, but in intermediate school in Hawaii, after my math teacher Mr. B saw my famed Bretney Spears talent show performance, he recruited me to join the dance team. I was offered the captain position, sight unseen. People just want me, girl.

Everyone was into Mr. B, too. All the kids had crushes on him. He was in his twenties and super cool. His car's license plate read PEMDAS, for "Please Excuse My Dear Aunt Sally," the order in which you're supposed to solve equations: parenthesis, exponents, multiplication, division, addition, subtraction. Mmmm-hmm, I still got it. That was so hot of him.

Anyway, Mr. B was all, "We need you, Bretman." Foine. All of my girlfriends were already on the dance team, so I'm in. Me and the girls relentlessly practiced our routine to "Next to You" by Chris Brown, which was definitely inappropriate. I knew we shouldn't have been dancing to it. But did I kill it? Yes, I did, especially during the line, "You will never go cold or hungry." How do I remember this like it was yesterday? I have an elephant brain, I'm telling you.

Bitch, I was so good at dancing. I was all set to perform center stage for Winter Carnival when fate intervened. During lunch one bright sunny afternoon, I was working our carnival fundraising booth in the cafeteria when suddenly the dreamiest teacher at school, Mr. Knee, approached the booth. No, it was not a kissing booth, girl, lemme finish. Mr. Knee always reminded me of Paolo Montalban, the Filipino American who played Prince Charming in the POC version of the movie *Cinderella*, you know, the one starring Brandy. How dreamy was Mr. Knee? If he were standing outside my door right now, years later, and asked me, "Would you leave your life for me?" Bitch, bye. Anyways, he taught science, my favorite subject, and he taught frog dissection in a classroom that overlooked our dance rehearsals. I know he could see me, and I definitely saw him. One day Mr. Knee came up to the booth and asked, "Do any of you guys want to join the soccer team?"

He was staring right at me. I was convinced he wanted me and only me.

I thought to myself, Mr. Knee, just be honest with your feelings. Come on, Mr. Knee. Girl, I see you peeking out the window, watching me dance from there.

Instead, I just giggled with my hand over my mouth and turned away bashfully. Oh my God, I'm falling in love all over again, reciting the memory. "Does anybody want to join the soccer team?" Mr. Knee asked again. Then he touched my motherfucking shoulder. I melted.

I'd never wanted to play a sport with balls in it after Pony League, but do you know what I did when I went home? (Get your mind outta the gutter.) I turned my piggyback upside down and took out every motherfucking coin. Then I went to the Coinstar, traded in all my coins, and went to Sports Authority with $20 burning a hole in my pocket. Howevuh, new cleats were $85, period. So once again I got to work. I had $20 from doing yard work for my uncle. I borrowed $25 from my sister. My mom gave me $20. And not only did my brother give me $10, that bitch got in his car and drove me back to Sports Authority.

Tell me why I got recruited for soccer right at the same time I was supposed to perform my Chris Brown interpretative bop? The gag is, I'd never played soccer in my whole life. I was just there for the dicks. Including Luke, who was on the soccer team and the cutest boy in my class and the crush of my grade. He was that kid. Everybody was hot for Luke. So before we even got to competitions or performances, I bailed on the dance team. I was like, "Yo, I'm too good for this. I need to try something that I'm actually not good at."

Get some popcorn and settle in, girl. Luke was in my home-room and a star student. He sat right across from me, and we bonded over sports. I was gay as fuck, but we had soccer to talk about now. We complained about how we had to run around the track for an hour straight for conditioning. "I can run for an hour but not in circles. Bitch, that's got me all kinds of fucked up," I'd say, and Luke would laugh and laugh. I wasn't kidding though, after my third lap, my boredom would kick in and I'd be like, Girl, why the fuck am I running in circles? I'm tired of looking at the same shit over and over again.

I was already busted-ass broke after buying my cleats, but I didn't know I needed long socks and shin guards, too. I had no money left to buy them. "Luke, do you have extra socks and shin guards?" I cooed. "I forgot mine at home." Luke came through for me. I wore his extras, with his sweat on them and everything.

Fast-forward two months, I realized I was actually good at soccer, and I was in heaven being in a Mr. Knee and Luke sand-wich. I was torn between two love interests and feelin' fine about it. But if I was forced to choose at gunpoint, I only had my eyes on one thing and one thing only, and it was still Mr. Knee. We had such a loving, healthy relationship and excellent communi-cation. Communication is so key in any relationship, wouldn't you agree?

"You're going to practice today?" he'd ask me as we swept past each other in the hall.

OMG, not you checking up on me, making sure I'm coming to practice. "No, I'm *not* coming to practice, *make me*," I said.

We were so cute . . . until Kevin came along. His name triggers me still to this day, the most obnoxious bitch in the world. He sucked at playing soccer, but he thought he was so good. I was like, Girl, how am I just playing this for forty-eight hours and you've been playing this since the beginning of your motherfucking life, and you still can't hit a goal or hit straight. And you *are* *straight*. We had a natural beef. One day we had a scrimmage, and Kevin really thought he was the star player that day, trying to run circles around me.

"Kevin, do you know that if you google defense, a picture of me is going to fucking pop up? I invented defense, bitch." I defended my motherfucking goal, and I did what I had to motherfucking do. I had gotten so heated that I took it a little too seriously, a little too far past my limit. I slide-tackled him. Everyone on my team was cheering me on like, "Go, go, go!" Even Luke was like, "Wow!"

But Mr. Knee. He turned on me.

"Bret," he said sternly, with zero emotion, "It's time to go home. You're playing too rough."

It felt like he'd chosen Kevin over me. I was ashamed, and I was heartbroken—I never showed up to practice ever again.

After Mr. Knee and I broke up, it was cold shoulders 24/7 from me. When he came into a room, I would go out. If he was talking to people in the hall, I pretended like I was checking my locker. Years passed—they say time heals all, and they, those motherfuckers, are right. My heart healed, but it never forgot.

One day in a high school science class I was making a bridge out of toothpicks when the ghost of Mr. Knee rose like a phoenix from the ashes.

"Did you ever have Mr. Knee in eighth grade?" my science teacher, Bret Kim (aka Mr. K), asked me. He was so cute, too, but I couldn't fall in love with someone who had the same name as me. Hearing my old beloved's name made my stomach drop and my heart burn with a passion I hadn't felt in ages. "I did have him," I told Mr. K, then paused for dramatic effect. "But only for soccer."

"I'm not going to be teaching next year," Mr. K continued, ignoring my sexual inuendo. The whole class gasped. *Mr. K is not talking to you, he's talking to me*, I hissed inside my head to my classmates.

"You're not teaching next year?" they all cried like little bitches.

He told us he was going to be a firefighter . . . with Mr. Knee.

Well, well, well. I haven't mentioned this yet, but being a firefighter is my endgame, too, wut the fuk. When the spotlight fades and my millions of followers and fans scatter into the wind, I plan on getting the training and taking the test to become a hose ho. (God, wherever flames may rage, give me strength to save a life.) Someday I *will* be meeting up with Mr. Knee again. Put money down on it. Plus I already figured out which station house Mr. Knee works at.

So that was a really long tangent, just to tell you that I played soccer for one quarter. But I felt in my heart and my loins that you really wanted to hear that story.

Sports, to be honest, wasn't really an emotional outlet for me (I mean, clearly it wasn't helping with my outbursts of frustration) until high school, when I got super into track. I was already pretty stressed out from my increasingly successful influencer career. My life was pretty absurd for a high schooler. In eleventh grade, I'd gone on a big tour with other social media influencers (who even does that?), but even with all the travel and attention, I stayed focused on school—I would graduate high school with honors. I did my homework on planes and did squats during fucking first class to keep in shape for the track team. Track became my escape, and the endorphins helped manage my ADHD by keeping my mind from overthinking. In track, you're either fast or slow. I happened to be very fucking fast, and even went to the state championship. And don't get me wrong, I love winning—my dad didn't raise a loser—but more important, on the track team, I learned that your real competition is always with yourself. When you think you can't do it anymore, it's all up to you to decide whether or not you keep going. Track also taught me not to run in the rain, or you'll get sick the next day. When I run, I can leave everything behind as my dainty feet hit the pavement. I never think about my destination. I get to forget this chaotic world that we live in. I think that's the true beauty of running.

Track was my healthy outlet at that time, but at the peak of my running career, I also found weed. Well, the first time I actually found weed was in my dad's closet when I was eight years old, but I started smoking it myself my senior year. I hadn't smoked weed my whole life up until that point. I feel like people think I've always been a stoner, but no, it's only been for a few years.

I'm not sure if weed actually made me faster, but I do think it made me a little more paranoid, because as I gained more and more notoriety, I wound up quitting the track team. I became really

Me at my seventh-grade track competition

insecure, and I didn't want anyone to watch me run anymore. Being a perfectionist, I also had become more and more scared of losing.

When I stopped running every day, my pussy got really fat, because after I became a stoner, I started getting the munchies and eating a ton. For many people, this seems like an unfortunate turn of events, but not for this bitch. Eating a lot was a good thing for me.

I've never talked about this before, but the only body image issue I've ever had has been struggling with an eating disorder. I'm pretty sure I had one then. I wasn't diagnosed with it, but there was definitely a time when I was younger, when I was hardcore blaming myself for my parents split, that I'd purposely tried to eat as little as I could in a day as a response to trauma. I used to tell myself, *Don't eat,* or I would refuse to eat or joke around with my auntie about how tiring chewing was, and get away with not eating. Everyone in my family will tell you, as a kid, I barely ate after my parents separated, even though I was running around constantly doing after-school activities. I don't know how I didn't collapse. I think I just got used to it.

My mom was even a whole-ass cook. Maybe in some ways, I didn't think I deserved her food because of what I did to her. Again, this is the kind of stuff that's hard for me to think too deeply about, and stuff I'm still working through. I can see now that I had been using track, and then weed, to try and cope with stress. In a lot of ways, I think it was a good thing that the weed caused me to start eating like an animal. The munchies triggered what I call my masculine era. Before weed, I was muscular but skinny, and after, I was able to gain fat and muscle from eating more. Bulking season, as it were.

When I first started gaining weight, I was wearing these blue pants that made my ass so scrumptious, and someone shouted out, "Bret, your ass is so fat!" That was the first time I'd ever gotten that compliment. In that moment, mental health and body image issues vanished from my mind. Somebody said my ass was fat.

I'm pretty sure it was one of my thicc girlfriends who first said it, either Justice or Dream, because ever since that day, we'd always refer to ourselves as the Thicc Girls. And I kept eating after that, especially. I liked being called a Thicc Girl. If I turn around in a photo, my ass takes up the whole pic. It's so exciting!

I was also excited when my metabolism evened out a little more after I hit puberty. I started to broaden. The only downside I can see during this time is that I got kinda lazy. Sloth had never been part of my personality before that. Then one day I was lying on my couch eating garbage and watching Netflix when I stumbled on a documentary about CrossFit. It pumped me up and reminded me how much I really missed running track, and that being active is also a stress-relieving escape from the real world.

So I tied my shoelaces and went for a five-mile run. I was dead as fuck afterward, but I loved it.

I've worked out every day since.

For a long time I did CrossFit three times per week, and weightlifting another two times. Now I just make sure I get two arm and leg days in and at least one cardio a week. I have a work-out itch. If I don't work out, it actually eats me alive. I hate to admit this, but there are definitely times where I get out of bed in the middle of the night to do an hour workout because my brain is like, *Bitch, you didn't do abs today. You got to go do abs.* Sticking to a schedule has definitely become a coping mechanism, and a way of feeling like I'm in control of my life. I still experience the effects of ADHD, but sports helped me find a way to exert my energy and manage my stress and emotions differently than how I used to.

I post myself working out shirtless a lot because yes, bitch, my abs look foine and my ass is so juicy in my workout shorts, but I also think it's important for everyone to have self-love and prac-tice self-care, especially genderqueer, nonbinary, and trans peo-ple, who may "hate" the bodies they were born in. Your body is enough, but you should move it sometimes too. Michelle Obama taught me that. Even if you don't want a six-pack, at least go on a walk.

When Nike asked me to be a model and ambassador for their "Be True" campaign for Pride Awareness, it was one of the highlights of my life. For my main photo, I was jacked up but also wore a sports bra and a pastel scarf. I looked hella fit but also femme. I truly believe strength has no gender, it's a measure from within. Being seen the way I've always wanted to be in this campaign was such an honor.

I love my feminine curves, but I also love being strong and butch. I love that feeling of knowing that I'm strong, not just mentally but physically, too. I think I got away with looking a little bit more feminine throughout my earlier years because obviously I was skinnier—it's a little bit harder to hide these arms these days. So now I'm a pretty face with arms and a thick little tush.

I love the quote "My body is my temple." I burn incense before every workout, and I lay out all of my crystals right in front of me. I do a meditation. After every workout I burn palo santo for spiritual purification and energy cleansing.

I don't show that part of my ritual because I don't want people to think I'm weird. But I do see it as an extension of a spiritual practice. Working out is so much more than sweating and sculpting your body. It's a time to really be with yourself, appreciate your mind and body, and test all of your capabilities.

···

Tips on Caring for Your Own Hot Bod

A lot of my friends have body dysmorphia, and a lot of them are models, and they still don't love their bodies. But I just want to remind you to stop comparing yourself with anyone else, because ain't no one cuter than you. Once you realize your competition is only with yourself, you'll realize it's just about you and your own finish line. I've learned to celebrate every part of my body, the good—my perfect cheekbones, beefy biceps, and freshly plucked legs—and the bad, like my acne scars, stretch marks, and even my lazy eye. (Just know while my left eye is steering, the other is gripping your thighs.)

And remember, a lot of what you see when you see photos of beautiful people on your phone are perfect poses, good lighting, excellent editing, and sometimes . . . a little Facetune. If you want to feel as beautiful as what you see—have a photo shoot yourself! Go wild with the lighting and styling and glam and remind yourself that with a little bit of work, we all can look like what we see on social media

TEN

It's Not You;
It's Your Penis

There are Twinks and there are Twonks.

I feel like now more than ever, people associate me with the word Twonk—a hunky Twink. During high school, I graduated from Twink to Twonk, and I haven't looked back. And as a Twonk, I am bombarded with dick pics daily. This is not a humblebrag, it's a fact—thirsty guys slide into my DMs on the regular. I need to make something crystal clear: stop sending me nudes, I am not interested in your crusty dusty dicks that look like a dry ass rat! Periodt.

Because I happen to be an international sex symbol now (if being cute is a sickness, then pray for my recovery), I feel like people get the wrong idea about who I am when it comes to matters of the heart and head. Also, it's extremely rare for me talk about my dating/sex life on social media, which only adds to the confusion and mystery around who I am as a seggsual being. Here, for the first time ever, I will share all of the twists and turns on the path to my sexual awakening. The journey has been littered with broken dreams, shattered hearts, and loosened holes, but I want to dig deep to explain just exactly who the fuk Bretman Rock is as a lover.

Let's go back to the beginning: I realized while writing this book that I've kissed more girls than guys. Don't get your panties in a knot, I am still 100 percent a gold-star lesbian because I've never had sex with a girl! But straight activities had me fucked up in my early days. According to the rules and regulations of the Council of Fashion Designers of America, I've had two real girlfriends. The first one was Melony, remember, our neighbor girl back in the Philippines that everyone always teased me about getting married to. When I moved to America, I was still in denial of my sexuality. Everyone was well aware that I was, let's say, *girlie*, and that my gender was, shall we say, *gay*, but that early on nobody knew what my sexuality was. (This is a pop quiz: are gender and sexuality the same thing? No, bitch, da fuk?) And my second, who I also mentioned earlier, was this tomgirl in my homeroom named Jasmine.

She didn't even like me, she didn't even want to be my friend, and everybody wanted to be my friend, so I think what attracted me to her was mostly the thrill of the chase, and that she was a cool chick. I told my girlfriends that I had a crush on Jasmine, and you know them bitches had loud mouths and they told her. Before I knew it, I'd made a poster for this bitch, like those scientific threefold posters, and I put WILL YOU BE MINE in big letters before opening it at lunch in the cafeteria in front of God and every kid in that school. Girl, I invented the Promposal—before that it was just basic-ass pen and Post-it note under the table, "Will you be my girlfried? Yes or no?" type shit. Jasmine said yes (even though this punk-ass bitch named Jaden tried to ruin the moment by shouting out, *"I thought he was gay!"*), and I made the whole school sign the poster for her.

I've had foundation that lasted longer on my sweaty face than my courtship with Jasmine. Around Christmastime, people tried to get us to kiss under some mistletoe, but I was not having it. That is so fucking gross, I thought. Like I would never. (Hello, that was a big clue.) And after never even so much as holding hands, Jasmine had the audacity to ask me to meet her brother. "This is too soon," I cried. What was she thinking? There was no way I could meet her brother, cuz I was scared that if I fell in love with Jasmine, and she was a girl, I could only imagine how handsome her brother was. I didn't wanna fall in love with him, too. (That should have been another big clue.)

I broke up with her by saying, "Jasmine, my mom found out about us, and I'm not allowed to have a girlfriend. Bye." Even though my mom literally could not give a fuck and probably would've laughed like a hyena if I told her I had a girlfriend at the time.

I tried. I really tried before I came out officially to everyone! I had a girlfriend in the Philippines. I had a girlfriend in Hawaii. After I came out publicly by starting to wear makeup to school in eighth grade and after I started to become famous, I wish I could say I was drowning in seggsy time afterward. But nothing changed. I lived on a rock in the middle of the Pacific Ocean, population eight gay people. I was still the only gay boy at my school, the only out gay boy that I knew of on the island at the time, and

P.S., everyone was still ugly. I couldn't even find action outside school. One time I was waiting for food at a restaurant, and a cute guy asked me for my number. I really thought I'd found the love of my life. Next day a girl hits me up like, Hey, can you do my makeup for my sister's wedding? So I stayed single until the end of high school, although there was one notorious straight boy who wanted to experiment with me . . .

Freshman year, after Mr. Knee betrayed me, I walked into my homeroom class and this one kid Clark told me I had nice blue pants—and I fell in love with him immediately.

Girl, I remember everything about Clark. Born June 10. We had every class together, and he sat next to me on my right.

Every day I sashayed past Clark as Tyra would have instructed me to, smized, and sat sideways in my chair on porpoise, to make sure he saw me at all times. It was very Beyoncé "Rocket" c. 2013, "Let me set this asssss on you instead." We had cute pet names for each other. He called me Burger King Bretman and I called him Jamba Juice Clark. His football jersey was #21 freshman year and #11 every year after that. We played badminton together in gym class. No other straight boy wanted to be on my team or be my partner, but he didn't care. When we played catch, he'd throw the baseball as hard as he could at me, and I'd catch it every time. That's how sports people flirt. I'm sure of it.

And then, the day a single compliment would make me his forever (or at least until the end of high school): I was wearing dark turquoise jeans and Clark said, "Bret, where did you get those pants from?"

"Oh, I just got them from Ross," I clucked.

"I like them. They're kind of nice."

Clark made sure to flatter me again when class ended. "I *love* your pants, Bret."

Not liked. *Loved.* He knew a good bottom when he saw one.

I knew he loved them because they were the same color as his RVCA bag. We were color coordinated, like vintage Cardi B and Offset. We were soul mates, obviously. We were a love story for the ages.

Record scratch. The truth was, in hindsight, Clark wasn't even flirting, I'd become obsessed with him, but he was just being nice because that's how he was to everybody. And that was what was so attractive to me. Not only was he nice to me, he was even nice to the bitches I didn't like in class, like Viviane and her loud mouth. I was like, Wow, this is someone who sees the silver lining, the beauty, in people.

Clark was my biggest high school crush, and everybody knew it even though I really wasn't talking about it openly. Even my English teacher would ask me about him. I think LGBTQ+ kids, especially ones who live in small towns, conservative areas, or a motherfucking island in the middle of the deep blue sea, don't really let themselves think that seriously about relationships during school. We only have a small pool of prospects to choose from, like a kiddie-size pool, if even a fucking pool at all. So a lot of us spend our formative years feeling left out when it comes to love. We don't get asked on dates, we don't get to ask other queer people to proms, or even get to fumble around awkwardly in the dark hooking up with our crushes and learn how to smash through trial and error—or at least, I know I didn't. I think straight people take that for granted.

It's getting better for the horny queer teens out there today, but back in my day, by my senior year of high school, I was ready to fucking explode. It was time for this girl to get some serious action!

Right after I turned eighteen, I was invited to an Instagram event at VidCon, which was held at Disneyland that year. They rolled out the red carpet for us influencers—we had chauffeurs and beefy security guards and they put us up at one of their fanciest hotel properties. I was the Kween of Con, the belle of the ball. I was really feeling myself, and the event itself felt charged from the minute I got there. While I was being escorted around behind the scenes, I saw an X-ray of Disneyland. The real underbelly. I heard all of the Disney characters talking in their real voices and saw Tigger and Goofy making out. I witnessed Minnie Mouse smoking a blunt and Elsa grabbing Donald Duck's pantless ass. (Okay, maybe this is just part of my furry fetish acid trip fantasy, but I'm sticking to it.)

Moments before becoming a Disney star

Seeing how the sausage was being made kinda ruined Disney for me, but the whole trip wasn't a loss. I mean, drum roll please: I lost my virginity at the Happiest (and Horniest) Place on Earth. Here's how it went down: I was walking around the park with my influencer group and craving a churro so badly. I ditched them for a hot minute and snuck into a long line at a churro stand. A cute boy, also longing for a big hot fluffy churro, recognized me.

"You're Bretman, right?"

"It is I," I replied with a curtsy. Bitch, I don't know, I was high, so I can't remember everything perfectly. The boy laughed. He was cute—a light-skinned Dominican in his early twenties. He asked for a picture, and I complied, of course! But my group started moving on—I had to forget the churro, but I didn't want to forget the boy. He'd given me some feels . . .

That night, back in my hotel room, I was hungry cuz I couldn't get the churro and thirsty cuz I couldn't get the boy. I downloaded and opened up the Grindr app on my phone for the first time ever, because all my LA friends had it and were doing it, and literally, immediately, there was Churro Boy staring back at me. My phone made the *BOO-DOOP* sound, and I got a message:

Hey, I don't want to make it weird, but I'm the one who asked for a picture at the churro stand earlier. I think you're pretty cute. And sorry for asking for a picture. I didn't know how else to approach you.

I looked at the location thingy. He was 900 feet away. We were staying in the same fucking hotel.

"What are you doing right now?" I tapped back. Oh my, I do declare, who *was* this new, seggsually bold Bretman Rock? A dramatic pause . . . "I still need my churro."

Obviously, I was there with VidCon, and I knew I probably shouldn't try to bring people to my room because I didn't know if they had cameras on us. Buttttt . . . I did it anyways. It was time! I was sick of looking like a dumbass when all my girlfriends were talking about dick and I was just out there with nothing to share. It was very much just like, It's fucking time.

And oh honey, I got my big churro that night.

To be honest with you, when I invited him over, I didn't even think sex was gonna come out of it. I legit just thought like we were at most gonna play around and kiss and maybe sugg digg.

Let me remind you, I'd never done *any* of this before. At that point, I had never held hands with a boy or been that close to one. I had watched plenty of porn really early on because one of my babysitters played it on TV all the time like white noise (there are a lot of sickos in the world). She got some education, she got some lessons, and subconsciously some childhood trauma and whatnot. Still, I didn't actually know how to approach sex. I didn't know what could happen, but I wanted it.

The boy came to my room, and we got on the bed. My big move was asking him, "Oh is that a tattoo on your stomach?" Then he took his shirt off. What was that? All you had to do was lift your shirt up, bitch, you didn't have to take the whole fucking thing off . . . and then suddenly I realized, Oh my God, I will be getting fucked tonight. Yes, I will.

He gave me a tour of all of his tattoos, and then, next thing I know, I found myself kissing my first boy. It was so romantic . . . until the bitch started eating my ass. I was like, OMG, literally this is the first position? He had a little bit of facial hair, and I did not know how to get my ass ate, so it tickled so much, more than it felt good. I was so overstimulated I kept clenching. He wasn't mad, though.

He did his part, and then I was like, Girl, am I about to suck dick for the first time right now?

I'd gotten naked already while he was still in his underwear. At first it was not intimidating. But when he took his underwear off and I got my first look at his penis, I was like, Why is it *folded*? Is this a flip phone? Is this a taser? Bitch, am I being detained? Where does one begin in this journey? I was confused, but at the same time, I was ready. I was like, *You know what, Bret, you've watched porn. Some are even bigger than this. You can take this.* I started going Gluck Gluck 9000 (Urban Dictionary that, if you don't know what it means), and that's how I found out I was really good at playing the clarinet.

Unfortunately, after the blowie, it was intercourse time, and it was clearly obvious I was a bottom, duh, but it wasn't obvious to him yet that I was a virgin. He was about to find out though. How can I put this delicately? It was the opposite of throwing a hot dog down a hallway. (Mmm, hot dog, I was still hungry because I never got my churro . . .) It did not go down smoothly, girl. Or up, in, or out. Believe me when I tell you every attempt was an epic fail.

They always tell us queer kids, "It gets better." Bitch, that shit did not get fucking better. Every stab, thrust, and poke hurt. "Pull that shit out, pull that shit out!" I whimpered.

"It's just the tip," he said, surprised, then finally, "Are you a virgin?"

"No, no, I've just had island dicks my whole life."

That's literally what I said. I gay-panicked, and a horrible stereotype came flying out of my mouth. Like, he had an island dick, too—he was from the Dominican Republic, and his was the size and girth of a baseball bat. Shattering stereotypes, one penis at a time, yuh. Luckily, he laughed. And kept trying. We finally got it in, but then something else came back out with it . . . a meek fart, and then a small speckle of poop that fell on the bed.

. . . I've never even told this story to my friends.

Well, after I shit on his dick, it was time to wrap this party the phuk up. The phat girl had sung. After he ran to the bathroom to wipe off his dick, he was like, "Girl, it happens, and sometimes it's worse."

Fine, he might not have said "girl," but he was still very sweet and mature about my utterly disastrous virginity snatching.

Despite the international poo incident, I was flying high the night of my deflowering. But the day after is really when it all hit me. Not only did I feel so gross, but my whole body was physically wrecked. Like, my left leg didn't work for some reason, can someone please explain that to me.

The physical side effects of losing my virginity only lasted a couple of weeks—my hole's snap-back game was strong, it closed right up. But mentally, I was forever scarred. I remember the next morning staring at the wall, thinking, *Who the fuck is gonna wanna fuck this loose-ass pussy of mine now? Damn, nobody's gonna wanna fuck me now.*

I went big and then I went home. And then *for real for real,* I didn't have sex for a year after that. The good news is that once you experience titanic dick, there's nowhere to go but down from there. It's like how they say about New York City, if you can make it there, you can make it anywhere.

When I finally tried it again, I realized not all penises are monsters. My second hookup was this decent guy, Asian and Brazilian. And his dick was smaller, so I was all, *Okay, yes, NOT traumatizing dick does exist.* Honestly, the best ones are the smaller ones. A year after that, I was feeling very emotionally and sexually available and looking for love . . . or at least an afternoon delight. I'd finally figured out what I like—men who are older than me, and brown . . . sorry to say, I'm just not interested in white guys. I'm so scared of their penises because they're very pale and you can see through them, and when I can see the veins and it's purple, it's like oh my God, no I don't want that.

My choices still felt limited though. I didn't want to date a guy on my island—I did like going to places where gays were like, "Oh my God, that's Bretman Rock!" but I felt so cute being unavailable on my home turf.

I still threw myself into the dating app world in Hawaii and LA, and started meeting guys on Grindr and Tinder. I get hit on in my social media DMs a lot, but I'm also very cautious about dating via social media for obvious reasons. The apps were very icky and cringey. I love men. But I hate men as well. Grindr was basically shirtless torsos or legs or ass. I used such a cute pic, and all I got was dick pic after dick pic. Everyone's opening line is always "Top or bottom?" Bitch, how about saying good morning? People would send these messages always at the weirdest times, too, like 8:00 a.m. I still have eye boogers, and you're asking me if I'm a top or bottom? I have yet to brush my teeth, and you're already on Grindr? I mean I'm on here, too. Why the fuck are we both on Grindr at 8:00 a.m.?

Most people were there for sex, but I was there to be seen. Everybody was always serving body, but I always served face. I posted the best pictures of me. I was like, "This is my face. I'm nineteen. I'm 150 pounds and skinny. If you want me, come get me."

Dating apps were tricky for me, especially as a public figure. Every time you have to verify yourself with a person, I'm like, Girl, I'm already verified on the app. They're like, "Just so I know that it's you, can you send me a video?" What am I doing, giving out free Cameos now? However, if you're catfishing your crush on Grindr pretending to be me, I will help you. No joke, I have done this several times. The only problem I have with these catfishers is that they don't pick good pictures of me. I also hate when they catfish as me and use pictures from when I was younger. But if you need help, like if your sugar daddy doesn't believe I'm you, and wants a picture with, like, a fork over your head, just DM me. I will take a picture for you. I actually took a picture with a fork over my head to help someone, and that bitch said thank you but never updated me to tell me if it worked.

After I lost my virginity, I didn't have much luck dating for a while—everybody else, even these catfishers, seemed to be getting more action than me. I was super relieved that I had finally lost my V-card and gotten some experience, but I had yet to experience true love . . . but bitch, no one could have prepared me for my first time in love.

Douching Your Ass Like a Bad Bitch

If you're a bottom, you're gonna have to learn to douche correctly. I found that out the hard way (Fartgate), so I'm here to save you the embarrassment. I mean, even the hottest people have embarrassing moments, and you know what, when shit happens, at least you get a funny story out of it. But shit can be prevented. So now I have a whole routine, girl. Feel free to steal it before your next seggs session:

1. First things first, get the Neutrogena Pomegranate Exfoliating Face Scrub, periodt. But you're not gonna use it for your face. You use that as your first initial wash on your ass. Boys love the pomegranate scent and the bubbles.

2. Next, grab a douche. If you don't have a douche, you can use a regular water bottle, like Smart Water, that comes with a twisty top. But if you wanna be professional, like me, go to a sex store and get an actual douche.

3. Fill up douche with cold water. Always use cold water for the first two squirts.

4. Squirt the water up your bum and shit everything out. Do this as close as you can to a shower or tub or a toilet.

5. Repeat at least twice.

6. Once you've got like the first initial shit out, that's when I start getting experimental with douching. I mix a gentle Kiehl's lavender soap with water. Shoot the lavender water all up in your fucking ass until you only shit out water. Make sure whatever scent you use up there is the same scent shaving cream you used to shave your ass. I choose lavender. Drives the boys wild. You can't be having like peppermint shaving cream, then lavender. No, no, no.

7. Most of all, enjoy the process. If you and your partner do not do this, you will pay the consequences. I promise you that, bitch.

ELEVEN

Adulting Like a Motherfuxer

One time when I was around eighteen, after senior year of high school, I went on tour, and I had a meet-and-greet after every show. I met everyone for thirty seconds each, took pictures, and called them "bitch" if they were into that kind of thing. This one girl at my Texas show, I don't even remember her fucking name, was like, "I have a gift for you!" *Wink wink.* I get all sorts of gifts from everyone who comes to see me at every show. Food, stuffed animals, artwork, gift cards, vibrators. I didn't want to assume what the girl got me based on her winks because yenno, when you assume you make an *ass* out of *u* and *me*, but it vaguely crossed my mind that it could be an edible or something in the cannabis family.

Mind you, at this point in my life, I was still sort of a newbie in

147

the weed world. Remember, at the beginning of high school, I was a goody-two-shoes baby kid. While all my friends were high 24/7, I was a stone-cold straight-edge nerd. I was all into D.A.R.E. and believed Tony the Tiger when he said drugs weren't Grrrrrreat, they fry your motherfucking brain. I had this old-fashioned-ass mentality that weed was basically the same as meth.

I used to shame my friends—I'd literally say "Ew" when they lit up—but I would be their babysitter while they were high, and it became my job to be the funny kid who made them laugh their asses off. But it got boring being the clown, and as we all know, I don't do well when I'm bored. So one day, walking home from school, I finally gave in to peer pressure and was like, Fuck it, let me just take a rip of this shit. I took what I thought was the biggest hit of my virgin life out of a pink pipe with spikes. Then I went home and took the cutest nap of my life until sundown, and my mom had to wake me up.

Anyway, back to this meet-and-greet—I said thank you to the winky girl and moved on to the next bitch in line. Afterward, we just dumped all the gifts people got me into a suitcase. I took an Uber to the airport, checked my bags, and waited for my flight to depart. I was eating tacos in the VIP lounge when all of a sudden I was surrounded by cute security guards carrying one of my checked bags. Did a fan get me a stripper gram? How thoughtful. In my chaotic brain, I actually thought these bitches were gonna escort me to my gate, and was all like, Calm down, guys, I'm not *that* famous yet.

"Are you Bretman Rock?" said the *not* cutest one. I will never forget that.

"Why yes, Officer, do you need to frisk me?"

"Do you have anything in this checked bag that shouldn't be

on the plane?" Guess he was on his period and not in the mood for foreplay.

"I don't think so?"

"Do you have anything illegal?"

I paused and thought about it. My stomach dropped. That girl and her winks.

What if she really did give me weed?

Oh shit. Weed was still not legal in Texas. It was forbidden fruit.

"I'm just here for a tour, and fans give me gifts . . ."

Nobody was listening. Next thing I know I'm in motherfucking handcuffs, and not in a zexy way, being dragged through the airport like a common criminal. These coppers were the most dramatic fucking people I've ever met in my whole entire fucking life.

"I literally just shoved everybody's gifts into my suitcase," I pleaded. "Y'all are gonna find candies, letters, paintings of me . . ." I believe there was an eye roll or two from this.

Everyone in the airport was staring, not because I looked travel chic, but because they thought I was a terrorist. I was taken to the county jail and booked by another real cutie at the front desk. He had this energy about him—he was good people, I could tell. It was time to turn up the Bretman Rock charm. My personality was gonna have to get me out of this mess. I posed in front of him as seggsily as possible.

"What are ya in for?" he asked, as he perused my report. "Oh, it's marijuana, huh. Where do you even find marijuana here?"

"I was on tour," I said, then explained that I was a social media star, which he actually seemed to find interesting.

"Up this way to take your mug shot."

I tried to do my best smizing as Tyra taught me, but I wasn't feeling myself. "I think I'm too oily in that picture, can I do it again?"

"Okay, fine." He laughed, bemused. How many criminals had ever requested a mug-shot do-over? Not many, I'm sure, but I was 100 percent positive I was the first suspect to be granted the request.

"Do you have a tissue so I can blot my forehead and nose?"

He handed me a piece of newspaper. My second one was better, for sure, but something was still missing. I was being so picky about my mug shot, but for very important business reasons.

"Sir, I'm not even holding up a sign—like, how will people know it's me? Can I retake it, if this is going to be public record?"

Asking to take three mug-shot proofs had to be a world record. I was wondering if the officer had one of those little glass plates photographers use to look at contact sheets, but I didn't want to be too greedy. So I just asked: "Sir, can I take a picture of my photo? I'd like to make merch with this mug shot one day."

"No." But he was laughing at me still—I had him in the palm of my hand.

He printed out my mug shot for me. Then he took me to my holding cell, which was already occupied by a man who was jerking off under his foil blanket. If he had been cute, I would have been living out my jail fantasy. But no, he looked like Kate Winslet waiting to be rescued at the end of *Titanic*. A drunk lady who got in a fight was across the way, eating a Lean Cuisine.

"Sir, I believe I'm allowed a phone call," I said to the cutie cop.

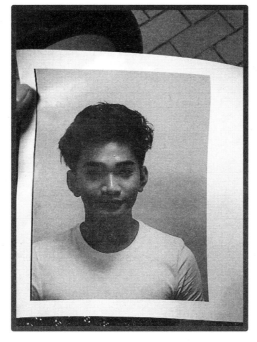

They caught me, girl . . .

"You do know this is not a real jail, right?"

I called my old manager and begged her to get me out of this prison, ASAP. She said it would take a couple of hours to figure out how to pay bail. A few hours? That couldn't be good for my skin.

The man was going for round two under his blankie, staring at me the whole time. My ADHD started kicking in, so I started doing squats, push-ups, and dips on the bench to pass the time. I wished there was a surveillance camera—I was dying to watch this back later. I'm not gonna say I was having fun, all I'm saying is that ultimately, this all started to feel like something that I needed to go through.

"Sir, do you have any food?" I hollered.

A girl gets hungry when she's doing hard time.

151

"What do you want?"

"I'm lactose, what do you have without milk or cheese?" Bitch, I had nothing to lose.

"We only have Hot Pockets."

"She had a Lean Cuisine." I pointed at the woman across from me.

"We only offer that to people who stay overnight—"

"I feel judged."

"If you leave me alone, I'll get you a Lean Cuisine and a Capri Sun."

"Two Capri Suns, and you have a deal."

See what you get for being annoying *and* charming?

The charges were eventually dropped, but this is still on my record, and I couldn't become a US citizen for another two years after that. Not that I wanted to, but I couldn't even if I did. All because of that gift from a fan.

When I got arrested, I knew I couldn't fall apart and cry in the corner of my cell like a pussy-ass bitch. I had to put on my big-girl panties and problem-solve. I managed to get myself out of a situationship with a creepy man, spring myself from the can with minimal damage, *and* get the cute cop's phone number. (That's a lie, he couldn't wait to get rid of me, but hey, if you're reading this . . .)

Because my family, for all that they loved me, has been so busy hustling to make ends meet my whole life, I've always had to rely on myself, and figure out how to adult all on my own—a lot of times the hard way first. I've been hustling to make money almost all my life (those chicken feather earrings, remember?), but becoming an influencer at such a young age took things to a whole other level that nobody I knew could teach me about. Getting out of jail was fun, but the business stuff had me all fucked up.

My very first real check came at age sixteen for $86.21, for giving people codes for teeth whitening pens. I gave a big fuck—that $86 might as well have been $86 million. I thought I was so rich, I showed my friends my PayPal account. I kept posting my code, and kept getting more money and followers—eventually I went from $86 to $2,000 a day.

When I first started earning money from social media, obviously I was still in high school, and the last thing I was thinking about was saving. Ew, that shit sounded so dorky. I kept my money in PayPal and wound up getting banned because I had too much money in that account, and then rebanned because I was underage. I'd called PayPal and told them my account had been frozen, and I didn't know why. Like a dumbass, I admitted I was under eighteen, and they permanently banned me. To this day, there's like $1,600 stuck in an account somewhere with my name on it.

After that, I wanted to be smart about my money, but yeah no, bitch, that didn't happen. I went through binge-shopping phases buying crystals, plants, and shoes. My very first paychecks all got spent on shoes and makeup. I was always envious of my friends over shoes because my mom would only ever buy us one new pair of shoes for the whole school year. Otherwise, we got shoes at Goodwill or the swap meet.

As soon as I started getting my own money, I was like, Bitch, I'm gonna need more footwear choices. I used to pick black Converse or black Nike Air Max for my one new pair of shoes a year because they went with everything. Now I let myself buy colored Converse, too—the first pair I bought, I chose red. Then I went to the mall and bought MAC makeup. I made a promise to myself then that every time I went to Sephora after that, I'd never leave empty-handed. That was my new rule. Shoes and makeup were the two things that I'd dreamed about buying when I didn't have money.

When I started earning even more, cars became my biggest extravagance. (Btw, I wanted a G-Wagon way before Kylie Jenner.) One day I was walking home from track practice, it started raining and I was like, Fuck this, I can't take it anymore, I'm done walking home—I need a car. Even though I didn't even have a driver's license, that night I bought a used car. I made my brother drive me to the nearest car dealership, and once I laid eyes on a 2015 Dodge Charger, I knew that was my car. I paid for the whole fucking thing in cash. I love big, manly muscle cars.

That same day, I picked up my friends in my "new" Dodge Charger, and we went to get boba. I barely knew how to drive. My brother tried teaching me once, but he was the worst. That bitch had no fucking patience. You know who taught me how to drive? YouTube (just kidding).

Actually, I first googled "How to start a 2015 Dodge Charger." Then I drove myself to 7–Eleven (illegally) and bought Hawaii's driver's manual book. Then I taught myself how to go forward and parallel park. And that was it. Bitch, within a week I got my permit. I got a really fast appointment for my test because if you're a bad bitch, you camp out on the website, refresh it at the crack of dawn, when you can snag canceled appointments. My friends were like, How the fuck did you do that so fast? And I was like, Girl . . .

But two weeks later I failed my driver's test. I wasted a perfectly good outfit. It was a see-through blouse moment—I was so cute. I was giving. I literally pulled up at the DMV smelling so good in my Dior perfume, Rose des Vents. It was totally lost on this salt-and-pepper-haired bitch who flunked me. I didn't give a fuck, I took it again two weeks later. I didn't even try with the outfit, and this time a bald bitch failed me again. Don't worry, girl, the third time was the motherfucking charm. Now this is when the term "the Bretman Rock card" was born, because the moment this lady saw me and said, "Bretman, my daughter loves you," I was immediately like, A bitch is getting her license today. We did a cute little lap talking about what I do and her daughter. Then it was time to parallel park. And I thought, Oh my God, this bitch is really gonna test me now. But the space was so huge I could pull in frontwards. She opened the door and looked at the curb. "That's twelve inches, you pass." Periodt. And that's how I got my license.

The only hitch was that I happened to get my license while I was testing out different highlighters. I thought putting on high-lighter for the test was gonna be a cute idea, but it wasn't. The number one lesson from that day was: Don't wear highlighter in your driver's license photo. Bitch, the fucking highlighter re-flected back the camera flash so badly that all you see in my driver's license photo are two reflective cheeks, a shiny-ass fore-head, eyes, and teeth.

Be grateful I'm telling you the lessons I learned, because no-body ever told me nothing about any of the systems here while I was growing up. Like nobody motherfucking told me about taxes. Not one single person. When I was sixteen and making my own money for the first time, I thought I didn't have to pay taxes. How was anyone gonna know through PayPal, the fuck? But it wasn't until I had really made bank that someone told me, "You're gonna

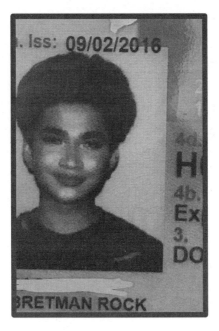

*Tip No. 1: Skip the highlighter
for ID pictures.*

have to pay taxes." And I was all, Who's taxes? I've never heard of her. She don't go to my school. She seems familiar, I guess, maybe I've seen her around.

I asked my mom about taxes, and she told me "they" send you this thing called a W-2. (Who da fuk is "they"?) Mine never motherfucking came because I wasn't working under anyone, I was freelance. Nobody I knew owned a business. Thankfully for me, I got the chance to ask about taxes when I was interviewed by a radio host at Power 102.7 Da Bomb. He was the only entertainer on the island I'd met at that point (pre influencer boom) who had the same caliber of fame I had. He told me to get an LLC, and he actually came with me to do it. He was an angel. But tell me why he stood by and watched me name my LLC "Bretman Rock,

Paper, Scissors"? Five years later, it's still funny, but I recently changed it to "Bretman Rock LLC," cuz it is slightly less embarrassing and I don't wanna have to explain myself.

I was so proud when I was able to buy my first house. (However, I did not know that electricity, water, cable, and mortgage were separate. I thought that you just pay for your house, and you're done.) I'm always dancing around alone in my house and bitches are always like, "Why don't you want your family living with you? You're so fucking selfish." I'm like, Bitch, you try growing up in a house with twenty-five people. I'd go to bed every night wishing I lived alone, and the next day even more uncles from the Philippines would move in with their wives and get them pregnant. Also, and this is none of your business, but since you comment without facts, I have helped my mom and my brother buy houses. Periodt.

As soon as I could afford it, I started living alone. I immediately adjusted to it. I want to live alone *forever*. I'm never lonely. I'm never scared. And I never want to live with anyone ever again. Not even a boyfriend.

Although, on second thought, it might be a smart idea to have a body around every once in a while to keep any eye on me. I've got a lot going on in my brain, plus the ADHD. Once, I forgot I was cooking rice and longganisa (Filipino sausage) and nearly burned my house down. It's not even like I was high. No, bitch, I just got sidetracked with a million tasks. Every morning, when I wake up, I stay in bed for twenty minutes and plan out my day, because I'm a busy little ho. This particular day, I'd cooked the rice and started boiling the longganisa, but I wasn't about to just sit there and watch water boil, the fuk. I went to pee, then I let my dogs Ele and Tora out. I looked at my grass and thought, "Oh girl, you're not looking happy today." So I started watering my grass, and it was so fun and meditative, I started watering the whole yard in little sections and squares. At this point, I'm on the other fucking side of my house. My dogs were peeing and pooping and then fucking Ele rolled around in peacock shit. I had to give my dogs a shower and thought, It'd be so cute if they smelled like lavender all day. So I went inside my house to get the lavender shampoo (yes, the same I use for douching, good question), and the whole place was on fire and smoky.

When the firemen came a-callin', all hot and bothered, I noticed that one was a cute butch I'd met at a gay club in town, and yes, girl, we had a moment—we locked eyes, but then I had to look away. Sorry, my heart will always belong to another firefighter, and his name is Mr. Knee . . .

Despite almost burning my house down once, I am a nice bitch who is slowly maturing and continuing to learn how to do responsible adult tasks. I learned how to get my oil changed, and I still make my bed every day. Girl, if you don't make your own bed, get your shit together! My mom said something once that stayed with me: "You're not gonna have a good day if you don't make your bed." There are times where I literally drive back home just to fucking make my bed. Full disclosure, I almost always still sleep on the floor unless I have, ahem, company, so there's not usually a bed to make—I just ruffle my pillow a little—but the sentiment still stands. That same house I almost burned down was eventually featured in *Architectural Digest*. Does it get any more grown-ass adult than that? It all started because I've always made my bed.

Listen, one adult thing I was taught to do well is taking care of things. Inanimate and animate objects. My dad used to make me take care of his animals back in the Philippines—dogs, pigs, fish, and I'd say chickens, but I was scared of his chickens. Flash forward to the present, and I basically have a zoo at my house. I have a parakeet, a peacock named Kym, a giant Sulcata tortoise, four cats, and four different pit bulls who I see as the four elements— Ele (my water girl, because she has a hook birthmark), Tora (my fire girl), Lila (my air girl, also named after my grandma), and Kayu (my earth girl).

L to R: Lila, Ele, Tora, Kayu, and more to come

I take good care of my human friends and family, too. One not so fun thing about adulting, especially when you start making bank, is that every bitch you've ever known will start asking you for money. I'm a giving person, but I have had to learn how to draw firm boundaries. Every time I talked to my dad on the phone from the Philippines, which was rare and only for about thirty seconds at a time after I moved to America, he always asked me for money.

Money has complicated all of my relationships. I hate that I know for a fact that people are just sitting around thinking about how much money I make. And I hate that people are calling themselves my cousins all of a sudden, or making up wild stories instead of just asking for help. Whenever I say no to money requests, their first defense is, "Well, you make so much." Bitch, would you like to tell me how much I make, then? Cuz I don't sit around thinking about how much money you make. When I can't help or don't want to, it's always my fault, or I'm the selfish one. When I give people money, I always try to give people advice, like, You don't really need my money, you really just need to find your own ways of making the money, and Bitch, if I did this shit myself, you can do it too. To be quite frank, I don't even know how much money I have, because I see numbers quarterly. I always tell my business managers, I would rather *not* see my money every day, because for someone who was broke their whole life, money means everything to me. If you remind me how much money I'm making, girl, I'm going act like how much money you tell me I have. If you tell me I made a million in a month, I'm gonna act like I made a million in a month.

Luckily, I have a great team around me. Again, I had to build my team myself at the age of sixteen, not having a fucking clue what I was doing. Even though I'm in my twenties now, I still feel like I'm cosplaying as an adult sometimes. Like, before I go to any family function, I like take a hit of my weed or eat mushrooms. You know, I'm still very much a teenage boy at heart, and I feel like my brain is still in college. (I don't have the patience to sit through actual college classes, even though I love learning. I just do it on my own through reading.)

I still do stupid shit all the time, often revolving around being

160

lit af. I'll do one thing adultish, like film a Logitech commercial with Lizzo in Vancouver, then get too high before going through customs on the way back into the US because I took an edible. Cannabis is legal in Canada, but there were signs all over the airport saying it's not legal to travel with it (I learned my lesson in Texas, y'all)—so in the check-in line, I ate all my edibles. You're only supposed to eat like 10 milligrams, and I had 30. Mind you, the last time I took 30 milligrams, I did not wake up on the plane. That's another story for another day. Don't let me get sidetracked, bitch.

So, since I still have a Filipino passport, US customs tend to pepper me with questions when I'm coming back into the country. This customs bitch was no different. He asked me what I did for a living, which has become one of my least favorite questions of all time. I low-key froze up because I was not about to say I was an influencer. Who says that? Last time I went through customs I told them I did YouTube videos, and they gave me a weird look. This time, "YouTube" slipped out of my mouth again, awkwardly.

I was stammering. I looked hella suspicious. Visions of Lean Cuisines and Capri Sun danced in my head, and I started shitting bricks and sweating profusely. I'm a sweaty, sweaty bitch, and don't you ever forget that. Listen, I was not about to go back to jail.

Thankfully the customs bitch was young, so he pulled up YouTube on his computer and searched my name. I didn't mind him watching me until he landed on a video of me screaming songs at Princess. I prayed he wouldn't pull up the one of me slapping my sister. He then asked to take my fingerprints, and I was so sweaty, my fingerprints would not read. We tried it four or five times on each hand, rubbed alcohol on them, put them under a fucking fan, nothing, bitch. The 30 milligrams were starting to hit hard. Was I even a human being, or was I an alien?

I was so worried I'd be detained, I literally shit myself. Well, more like sharted in my pantalones.

Because I was so sweaty and my fingerprints were invisible like a bad bitch, I had to be put off to the side until they sorted my situation out. I got called into a little windowless office, so I floated over, sat down, watched the walls closing in . . . and the first thing the new customs agent said was, "You've been arrested in Texas, huh?"

Girl. Thank God it was fucking freezing in there, because otherwise I'd have to rethink what I thought was the limit of sweating. "What did you do?"

"Oh, it was just for possession."

"What did you get caught with?"

"A joint? The charges got dropped."

"I'm looking right here, it didn't get dropped."

"Damn, bitch, I thought it did get dropped!"

He laughed.

I sobered up a little. It was time for the Bretman Rock charm school. I managed to sweet-talk his ass, after which he sent me right on into the United States of America, the greatest cuntry in the world.

When I was a free merman again, I told my manager that if there is anything I am thankful for in my life, it's my personality, because it's gotten me through so much in this life. This personality made me a millionaire. This personality got me a house. And this personality gets me through customs, bitch.

$$$ Management Tips

- Make and stick to a budget (girl, I know how hard that is).
- Pay with cash whenever possible.
- Pay your credit card bills in full. Don't rack up debt.
- Make your monthly bill payments automatic from your account.
- Get a savings account that you can't take $ from easily and try to put a small amount away each month (even $50 a month adds up).
- Look for a side hustle to make extra $.
- Have an emergency fund that is separate from your savings, just in case you need it.
- Never lend friends or family $ (but if you do, write up some kind of agreement on the payback plan).
- Get an app that tracks your spending and study it.
- Go through your phone and delete unnecessary games and subscriptions.
- Keep that credit score over 700.
- Don't ignore your taxes!!!!

TWELVE

That Front-Row Life

The first "real" showbiz gig I got hired for was as a red-carpet interviewer for the MTV Video Music Awards in 2017, hosted by Katy Perry. I met so many fucking famous people that night and was shitting my pants. I met the Dolan Twins. I was inches away from Khalid and Kendrick Lamar and Lorde and Shawn Mendes. I saw Jared Leto in a Gucci sequined cape. I was starstruck, genuinely frozen, completely out of character. They had cue cards for me that I couldn't even read, and I have ADHD, not dyslexia, bitch.

I looked so seggsy in a bare-chested number with perfect makeup, that was a given, but it was that red carpet where I realized that I am such a bad interviewer. I don't care who you're wearing. I don't give a fuck who you're excited to see. I don't even know who's fucking performing other than you, bitch. "I'm sweating and I'm from Hawaii, I should be used to this weather," I told some bitch in a leopard-print coat. I had no fucking idea who she was. Then for some reason I asked Dr. Drew what he wanted to say to all the teen moms out there. I pulled the buzzkill question out of my ass, and he was all, "Good luck and get help." Then I accidentally cut his hand with a pointy metal fingernail that was attached to my silver accent glove. But the hunky boys from *The Challenge* complimented me on my glove, so all wasn't lost (maybe just one of Doc Drew's fingers, sorry Doc!).

Then from my cute seat in the VIP section, I got to watch Cardi B perform "Bodak Yellow." I knew every line, and I was going off. I was still supposed to be interviewing people on Facebook Live, but bitch, how do you expect me to do that when Cardi B is over there performing, singing, "You can't fuck with me if you wanted to"? How can you focus and pretend like you give a fuck when she's doing that?

The second "real" showbiz gig I got hired for was hosting the Miss Universe pageant in the Philippines. That was my second and last event hosting any red-carpet show. I love beauty pageants (as every good Filipino does), and I love talking to the girls and about makeup—that wasn't the issue.

I was seventeen, and I was shitting my pants and sweating so much. But a news reporter ruined my debut. She was Filipino and asked me, "Why do you think you deserve to be here? Are you going to be professional enough to host a red carpet, and not swear?" It was so condescending—of course I know how to talk to people, and when not to swear. But I've always been sensitive about feeling like an impostor, especially because of the way I had to learn English on my own when I got here, and after years of getting called FOB a lot in school. I worked so hard on having the right American accent. It's such an immigrant experience where your home culture doesn't want to accept you for the things you had to do to survive, and criticizes you. Damn, bitch, I cried and blogged about it afterward. (It's on YouTube. Please don't watch it.)

After I figured out that interviews are truly not the right thing for me, I've manifested being on the other side of the camera only, periodt. Because I've always known deep in my soul that's where I belong. Always trust your gut. And before I knew it, I started to get invited to events that rocked my motherfucking world.

In 2016 a bunch of influencers got invited to the making of *Hairspray Live!*, and I was personally asked by Ariana Grande herself to hang out with her in her little trailer. It was such a flex that she even knew who I was. And it was my very first time in a trailer. I was so excited to see Ariana Grande, but to see that trailer—I was geeking out. As a baby entertainer, I'd dreamed of having my own trailer. I had already started making my rider list, too, girl. I'd always need orange Orbit gum, pistachios, Oreos, watermelon, eye drops—not for dry eyes, for red eyes—mints, and popcorn for my manager. I'm not about to get greedy and ask for flowers or a Bible or an air purifier. The fuk, you might as well be moving in at that point. Though maybe I will start asking for my monstera plant and a dog in every room . . .

So, Ari and I were kicking it, and she told me how much she loved me and introduced me to Daniel Chinchilla, makeup artist to the stars and one of my idols. Then Ariana gave me her number, which to me was the sign that I'd officially made it. A-list names in your contact list? That is the biggest flex of all.

Ariana Grande opened the floodgates. Next thing I know, all these celebs started following me on social media, like Lizzo and SZA. I started getting legit commercial endorsements, not just product shots. My business was booming—I elevated beyond sponsored posts and swipe-ups and started getting offers to be in commercials and write my own scripts for brand deals. I knew I was different than my peers so posing alongside products wasn't going to work—we had to build a business that catered to my strengths, and being funny just happened to be my recipe for success. In 2018 I filmed a Cover FX commercial with the one and only Chelsea Handler, whom I idolized because she'd invited 50 Cent on her talk show once, flirted with him on air, then dated him. That is exactly how I would host a show if I had one. I would only invite hot men on and flirt with them the whole time. Then I would make them ask questions about me.

When Miss Chelsea and I first met on set, the first thing I said to her was, "Chelsea, my mom loves you." (Why the fuck did I say that?) Then I was supposed to do her makeup, but I had to warn her, "I know how to do makeup really well—on me. I only know how to make myself look pretty. So, bitch, you're gonna look like me at the end." We immediately had a playful snappy rapport, even though I was shitting myself. This was the first time I'd actually been seated next to a celebrity who was not a fellow influencer or my sister, Princess. I wonder now if Chelsea hated me during all of this—I was fucking eighteen, still figuring out who I was and what I was, and didn't know how to talk to people yet.

These two pics are actually from a photo shoot for my ColourPop collab—I'm wearing glamified takes on traditional barong tagalog here, and a Filipiniana gown in the last pic.

But I must have had a big influence on her, because she wound up dating comedian Jo Koy for a while, who is Filipino. Coincidence? I think not.

There are seven billion people in the world, so it's a wild feeling when people, famous or not, know you and talk about you. It's weird to walk around and know that anyone on the street might know who you are—it's humbling to me.

In the beginning of my career, I was getting pretty famous quickly, and nobody in my life actually gave a fuck, which made me pretty sad at first. After the red carpet for Miss Universe or after a trip to LA to be at a rooftop party with all those skinny white boys from Why Don't We, I'd go back to school and the fucking teacher would make me do cafeteria duty, like serving lunch to bitches. I would be serving food, hoping for one person to at least ask me where I was and what I was doing—like, why was I wearing a pageant crown? No one cared that I was just at Miss Universe. The experience of feeling famous and then coming back home to feel like nothing was different was really jarring.

When Rihanna requested my presence at her mascara launch, though, I felt like I'd hit a turning point. Believe it or not, I was one of the first influencers to work with Rihanna's Fenty beauty line when she released her Body Lava at Coachella. I did it originally because I wanted the street cred, but then she noticed me through her Fenty team and wanted more of this bish Bretman Rock. It opened up a whole new portal into the world of Rihanna. I felt really VIP at her launch. I wasn't sure if RiRi was actually going to be there that night, but when I got this feeling that she might, I changed my whole fucking outfit. I was like, bitch, she will see me in a clean, all-black look, cuz I feel most confident in all black.

The night of, I got picked up at the hotel in a fancy black Escalade, and it took me to a house high up in the Hollywood Hills. Your favorite immigrant girl was wigging out, but I tried to keep my cool, even though *everyone* was freaking out—the energy in the room was about to pop off. I wanted to scream out, "Where's Rihanna? Where's Rihanna! You guys, I'm here for Rihanna!" But I kept the shouting just in my head.

When Rihanna finally actually pulled up, I was in awe. She breezed in, wearing a striking all-black ensemble with an off-the-shoulder leather jacket. She got the fucking memo, too, bitch. While she gave a speech about how Fenty mascara was back and better than ever, I turned to the random next to me and raved about how exquisite she looked. "I wonder what foundation she's wearing?" I whispered.

Rihanna paused. "I'm talking, Bret," she said, so Rihanna-ly, staring right at me, her emerald eyes piercing my soul.

When I tell you, I didn't say another word that whole night. *I shutted the fuck up.* If Rihanna tells you to shut the fuck up, you shut the fuck up. Suddenly I'm a sign-language expert. If I had something to say, I typed it on my phone and held it up like a modern-day Nell. Bitch, after Rihanna told me to shut the fuck up, I felt like I'd never talk again.

At some point, Rihanna went to a little product booth with a big-ass mascara wand to take pictures with her fans. Finally it was my turn, and girl, I was still afraid to talk, but I'd prepared a special monologue so many times, so I had to

I can't believe Rihanna met me.

speak: "Rihanna, I love you so much," I said quietly. I get really small when I'm around people I adore or when I'm overwhelmed. "Thank you for having me." That's what I'd rehearsed . . . twenty-seven times.

Rihanna just gave me that Rihanna look. *Bitch, stop being fake humble.*

Oh my God. I wasn't even trying to be fake humble. But guess what? When Rihanna tells you to stop being fake humble, bitch, you stop being humble in any way. We both started cracking up, and she told me her bestie back in Barbados was a huge fan of mine.

We went to take the picture, and I took a knee in front of her to show that she was a kween and I was her loyal subject. "I'm gonna sit on him," Rihanna said, and she sat on my little knee. I swear, I got a good whiff of Rihanna, and it smelled like rich puss. Rihanna has such a good scent, bitch, I know she's famous for it. I know you're gonna ask, so I'll tell you what it was like. If I could describe it, I would say the scent is like if the top florist in the world handpicked the finest roses and extracted the scent with the finest craftsmen tools. Rihanna smelled like pure roses with a hint of vanilla. Rihanna smelled like what you want your funeral to actually smell like. I've been to lots of funerals, and the roses smell like death. No, that bitch smelled like what your first step into heaven should smell like.

Obviously, Rihanna had other people to meet besides me— there was a huge line, and I wasn't gonna hold her up. It was fine, because I got the girlfriend experience: she sat on me, and her vagina was on my lap. Another memorable celeb meeting: breaking my shoulder right in front of my girl Megan Thee Stallion.

We were filming for her Snapchat show, and it was an obstacle course where we had to race with our dogs. At the mud-crawl part, we were supposed to put on kneepads first (that's what she told me!!), but Megan just dove in the motherfucking mud. We all know how competitive I am, so I was feeling that adrenaline of not wanting to lose because I'm a Leo: *This bitch isn't going to beat me.* Fuck the kneepads, I dove headfirst. Then I felt a *pop.*

I got into my plank position to start crawling anyways, girl, and I swear I felt full-on electricity throughout my whole body. My shoulder had gotten dislocated and was hanging off me like a yo-yo. Suddenly all the adrenaline was gone, and it was just pain. Everyone rushed to help me. I told the medic, "I don't care how much I scream, stretch my arm as far as you can, and I'll take care of it. Because you know what, I'm not about to look like a pussy-ass bitch in front of Megan Thee Stallion." He followed my directions, and I dead-ass popped that shoulder back into place.

Honestly I don't know how I knew how to do it, maybe from the times I used to just hang out in the trainer's room during cross-country and someone would pop their finger out of place and then get it popped it back in there, so I think I just channeled that.

Everybody on set was like, Damn, what the fuck?, and looked at me like I was some sort of superhero. I was in pain still, but low-key felt so cute. I ate that shit up. I got my street creds that day. All the straight men were in awe, like I was the most badass thing they'd ever seen. Listen, men want to be me and want me, I can't help it.

I'm happy about the bold-faced friends I've made on this wild ride so far, like Kehlani, a singer whose work I would say

*I love when my mom sends
me handwritten letters.*

helped raise me when I was younger—she was all I listened to when I was in high school. Kehlani's album *You Should be Here* was really very healing for me. Hers was the first live concert I went to. Now that we've become friends, she'll always message me about how proud she is to see how much I've grown as a person, as a soul, since we first met. I've always identified her as similar energy to me—masculine and feminine energy in a divine mix, like me. So for my idol to message these things to me, for them to truly see me—you have no idea, it feels so empowering.

I'm not obsessed with being famous for fame's sake. I would do what I do for free, I would do it for fifty million people following me, or even if I was only being watched by my mom and my sister. Fame can be tricky—sometimes I can still lose myself for

173

a moment, forget that I'm still a regular fucking human being, but then I remind myself to come back down to earth, girl. I live a very chaotic fucking life, but I always know when to ground myself and breathe, yenno?

Fame is a fickle bitch, and can turn on you in a heartbeat. For all of the success I've had, I continue to have humbling moments. Like, I haven't been invited to the Met Gala in New York City yet, and that hurts. Anybody who cares about fashion wants to be there. Part of me felt like I didn't get invited, didn't belong, especially since the theme for 2022 was "In America," and I'm a little immigrant girl. Whatever. I'll keep waiting. Until the next year or the year after that. I'm very patient.

There are also whole arguments online sometimes about how influencers don't deserve to be at Hollywood events, but fuck that, I worked so hard to be there. When I did finally get into the VMAs in 2021 and found myself standing next to Megan Fox, rumored to be a supernatural witch, I felt a pull from her—we looked at each other at the same time, and she winked at me. What do you do after Megan Fucking Fox winks at you? I'm gay as fuck, and even I melted. And it was a sign from a higher power that I belonged on that red carpet.

Bottom line is, I don't even like fame (except for the part where you can get new teeth for free). I still don't like calling myself a celebrity. One of the only reasons why I actually enjoy the fame aspect of what I do is that it helps feed my soul in more important ways, like getting to collaborate with Asian and LGBTQ+ designers and artists—representation is everything to me. The last time I was invited to New York Fashion Week I stayed the whole week and got invited to so many shows in every borough.

I got painted like a canvas by the best Asian makeup artists and dressed to the nines by my favorite iconic Asian designers. I went to the Saks party in this one-of-a-kind purple Robert Wun outfit that turned out so beautiful. That day, I embodied the essence of what I would imagine myself to be.

Then Peter Do dressed me the cutest in the crowd for his show at the pier. Everybody else was dressed in black and white, but I was in deep suede purple with red, giving nods to Prince and Michael Jackson. Seeing Peter's team, full of Asian faces and brown skin just like mine, was so powerful. The pictures they took of me at that show changed my life forever, just like my relationship with Peter Do changed my life. That week I also got dressed by Prabal Gurung, who is Nepalese, and Monse, whose lead designer is an Asian woman, Laura Kim. (She's so lovely. I love her smile.) It was just so inspiring seeing so many Asian faces during one of the biggest events in the fashion world. And there were also so many Asian photographers—it's cool too to see more faces that look like mine behind the scenes. I would still like to see more people in front of the camera, obviously, but it was all still so awesome.

I also got the opportunity to appear on a panel with legendary Asian designer Jason Wu, who talked a lot about dressing white people all the time at the beginning of his career. I could relate—when I first started creating content, I wanted to be accepted in the white world, too.

Sometimes I think a lot of people assume that because I'm an influencer, I'm illiterate. So during the first question I got from the host on the panel, I was nervous—I gave a short, sweet answer, and felt like I was coming off a little uneducated. Sometimes when I'm put on the spot, it's hard for me to directly translate in English what I'm thinking out loud. I gave myself a quick little pep talk in my head, then every time I did get a chance to speak after that, I tried to just be myself: I talked about being called māhū at school, and how my grandma always saw me as nonbinary. The audience started eating it up—I became the star of the panel. I didn't need fancy dictionary words to get my points across. I'm telling you this so you remember there are ways of changing people's perceptions once you stop subconsciously holding yourself back or self-sabotaging.

The real me, if it hasn't gotten across clearly over the course of this chapter, is not a phony starfucker. The real me is just a gurl who would rather hang with his family than a celebrity (but call me, Nas, for reals). After I shot a Logitech commercial in Canada with Lizzo, we didn't go clubbing afterward. I went to my favorite auntie's house in Vancouver because I hadn't seen her in eight years, and she made me my favorite Filipino dessert, houpia.

I was always low-key that auntie's favorite, too, growing up. Whenever my cousins wanted pizza, they'd say, "Bretman, ask auntie to buy a pizza," because she never said no to me. She actually always called me Baklâ, instead of Bretman. One time while my sister, Keiffer, and Colin were napping, I asked, "Auntie, why do you keep calling me Baklâ?"

"Why, you're not Baklâ?"

"Auntie, I am."

She was totally fine with it, she didn't care. We just laughed. If my uncle was like, "Hey, Baklâ!" to me, I'd be like, "Girl, that hurt." But my auntie was cool people and said it in a loving way. She can call me anything she wants as long as she doesn't call me late for dinner.

• • •

I don't feel the need to hang out with famous people . . . but I also still have fantasy friendships with celebrities. In my fantasy world, I'm best friends with BTS. Bitch, I've never even met them. But my nieces think I have because I'm famous. They think I Facetime with them and also BlackPink and Jennie all the fucking time. Girl. I let them believe it. I'll say and do what I want to keep my nieces happy.

There are a couple of famous people I DM all the time, and have never once gotten responses back. I guess I also just love feeling like a fan! You think I'm kidding, but I'm not—I have a full-on one-sided conversations with my namesake The Rock. I sent so many fucking messages and voice notes to The Rock, explaining how I was named after him and how I wanna do a movie with him so badly. I'll send him voice notes over Instagram, and once I even sang the lyrics to the Reba McEntire song "I'm a Survivor."

"A single mom who works two jobs . . ."

Yuh.

I can already see our movie poster: "Starring Bretman Rock and The Rock!" I'd be top billing, even though I'd play his assistant. I would genuinely love to have that moment, cuz I feel like it would also make it feel full circle for my dad who named me.

In actuality, I want to leave my idols on the pedestal. I'd rather pretend that I'm best friends with The Rock than actually be best friends with The Rock. I would die if one of these celebs did respond, not because it fulfilled something in me but because I'd actually rather them not know that I DM some of them almost every day. My biggest insecurity in life is for someone to find me cringe, so sometimes I get anxious and delete the messages I send people. But random people reach out to me, too, and I never turn my nose up, so I'm hoping the reverse is true . . .

When I first started, there was definitely a barrier between influencers and celebrities, especially when walking red carpets. They always made us go last, shoved us in the back behind the important people, and the paparazzi and bitches who worked the events went out of their way to make sure we knew we were nobodies. I mean, I knew my fucking place. I didn't think I deserved to step and repeat before Jennifer Aniston either.

But the line between influencer and celebrity is blurring, and I think my career has been proof of that. Back in the day, everyone thought the Kardashians were famous for doing nothing. Now they're worth billions, and I'm still not sure what they do, but it's not *nothing*. I started as an influencer, and I'm so proud of being a pioneer and paving the way for baby influencers everywhere. I've had conversations about this with colleagues who started around the same time as me, like Denzel Dion, Ricky Thompson, and Gwen Lane.

"Do you think we were prodigies of our time?" Gwen asked me once.

Now that I think about it—yes, we come from a generation of influencers who had to grow our audience organically in a time when no one knew what we were doing. The ball game was so different then. We made thirty videos a day. We had to do shout-out-for-shout-outs, we all showed up and worked VidCons as teens. We didn't have any templates for how to do this, how to monetize our work, how to have a sustainable career. So yeah, Gwen, I think we were legit. We were pioneers.

Ever since I became famous, I've been trying to evolve as a creative human being and entertainer. It's been a major learning curve, and there have been obstacles at every turn. Luckily for me, I was a motherfucking track star in school, so I know how to jump over hurdles with grace, power, and cuteness.

So don't be surprised if one day I tell you The Rock finally checked his DMs and sent me a voice note back, singing Reba McEntire: "But she's just too hardheaded . . ."

It could happen. Anything is possible if you manifest it, bitch.

How to Get a Celeb to Write You Back

I know I'm not alone. I know some of you bitches out there also DM celebrities. Getting a response is rare, but it does happen. I mean, I don't get a billion messages like Jennifer Aniston, but I guarantee she reads some of her messages. I get a lot, and I read most of them. I always write back to people who grab my attention in a positive way.

What I don't respond to:

- Mean comments
- Insecurity. Don't start with "I hope I'm not bothering you . . ."
- Asking for follow-backs or requests for money or shout-outs
- Excessive tagging
- Stalking. Please remember I am also a normal human being. Don't message me that you are "outside my hotel room." It's scary.
- Pussy pics. I want a man just as much as you do, but that's a little weird when I haven't asked for it first. Yenno?

What I do respond to:

- Original artwork (especially of me or my dogs)
- Funny memes or videos (especially about me or my dogs)
- Telling me if I have a booger in my nose in a pic or my fly is open
- Messages about causes I'm into
- Playful persistence
- Good energy. We are all so connected through our phones, and I really appreciate when people send positive or healing energy my way. Sometimes it helps more than you know.

THIRTEEN

The Bitches Who Made Me Who I Am Today

There are so many cultural influences, a perfect storm, if you will, that created "Bretman the Entertainer," from every corner of the earth, from every color of the rainbow. I feel fortunate that I grew up in Hawaii. A lot of brown and Asian groups migrated or were brought over to Hawaii to work for the white colonizers, and obviously when you put that many minority groups together, they're gonna have to fucking communicate cuz they're gonna be coworkers in the fields and shit like that together. So they had to mix words with English and created a language, pidgin, just to communicate with each other.

American and Hawaiian immigrant culture shaped me a lot.

But it's one thing to be Filipino American, and another to be an American Filipino. I was a Filipino first before I was American, and then there are Filipinos who were born in America, yenno? The cool thing about growing up in Hawaii, though, was that it didn't feel like there was a racial divide. It wasn't like *Mean Girls* or any of those cliquey movies, like you can't sit with us. But there was a division between recent immigrants versus the ones that were born here. Who's holding a blue fucking passport, and who's holding a red one? People would make me feel bad for not knowing that much English. I'd be like, "Miss girl, our families are from the fucking same city. How are you gonna fucking shame me when your mom probably knows less English than me?"

As I've mentioned, when I first moved to America, Beyoncé, Shakira, Tyra Banks, and Tila Tequila taught me not only how to speak English but also how to dance, how to feel art, fashion, and music deep in my soul. One of the music videos I remember the most was for the Cassie song "Me & U," where she dances in front of a mirror in her video. I would always run home from school to dance to Cassie in front of the mirrors, the wall behind me covered in paint splatters.

On TV, most of the people and characters I looked up to were women, and women of color. I always rooted for the women first, even if I was just watching her eat a motherfuckin' bug on *Fear Factor*. Actually, I would always root for whoever looked like me first, so the Asian girl always. We had to pay extra on cable to watch the Filipino channels, so there were never Filipinos or boys that looked like me on-screen, let alone like gay Asians that wore makeup. For a while, I was so used to not seeing me on-screen.

It wasn't until YouTube came out and Tumblr got big that I really started seeing myself—all these Asian women doing beauty tutorials, Ryan Higa—and then all these Tumblr pages that were literally called like, *fuck yes sexy asians*, reposting, you know, for the lack of a better word, sexy af Asians. So I was like wow, I don't see myself on TV, but I see myself a lot on my cousin's computer (cuz I didn't have my own computer). I was fine not being on TV then—even though there were Asian girls on *America's Next Top Model*, they'd never name one Asian winner. But YouTube—I was like, Oh my God, Michelle Phan is putting egg whites on her face. I'm gonna put egg whites on my motherfucking face. Ryan Higa is talking pidgin—he's Asian, he's from Hawaii, and he also speaks pidgin.

Then thank fucking God I found *RuPaul's Drag Race*. The first time I scrolled to it on the TV guide with the remote, I thought it was NASCAR racing. For some reason I clicked on it anyway, maybe cuz those drivers wear cute jumpsuits, and, I'm not exaggerating, it changed my life forever. It was the first time I'd ever seen drag queens. The first thing I saw was the scene when Manila Luzon and Yara Sofia were bouncing on a yoga ball in leotards. Then it cut to Manila Luzon doing a confessional out of makeup, and the record scratched. This Bitch looked like me. A gay Asian man in makeup, fxcking with gender. And her name was Manila? Like the capital of the Philippines? I didn't have to think twice, I was in love. She made me feel like a warm beacon of light enveloped my entire being.

I could tell you who won each season of *Drag Race*. Name a girl, I will give you her season. I know it like the back of my silky soft hand. I picked up a lot of Bretman lingo from RuPaul, too.

The cursing and my filthy mouth, though, came from my mom, period. She cursed in English and Filipino, so my mind was constantly translating things. Even if my mom just needed the fucking remote, she would have already said two bitches in two different languages before making the actual ask. I also grew up with so many rowdy uncles who cursed left and right in pidgin, *and* made up their own curses too, bitch. Add the influence of *Bad Girls Club*—the words my ears were selectively hearing the most in English were probably *fuck* and *bitch*.

What I didn't know growing up was that much of the slang and culture I was picking up while I was growing up, from reality TV to fashion and music, was Black culture, or coopted from Black culture (like much of the language around drag in *Drag Race*). For a time I truly didn't know that some of the words and phrases I used most in English were stolen. But it doesn't matter whether I knew this at the time. It matters that I know now and that I have addressed it personally and in public, as best I can.

So much of who I am—how I think, how I talk, how I see the world—has been shaped by Black and queer culture. How I sound online is not a gimmick. I understand it might feel that way sometimes, but whether in English or Ilocano, I have the same tone. But now I have a better understanding of where these influences come from, how to acknowledge them, and how Black and queer history have shaped so much of pop culture and entertainment today—and the history of non-Black folks monetizing their culture. A lot of Black women and Black queers support me and cheer me on, and I'm grateful for that. But I also continue get a lot of callouts from Black people. I wore an Afro wig in a video once, and didn't know it was appropriation until I was educated on Black women's hair. When the Black community does call me out for some reason, it never feels toxic. Since that first callout, I've continued to educate myself, to take time to soul-search, understand the criticism, and try to continue being the best Bretman I can be. I'm gonna continue to say sorry. Now, I understand that Black queer femmes fought for the fucking rights I have today, at Stonewall, throughout history. I'm not saying it was only Black queer femmes, but I owe so much of my rights and equal treatment as a gay POC here to queer Black femmes.

It does bother me when I get random comments that I'm a bad person, and uninformed criticism. I've been accused of darkening my skin on purpose, and of Blackfishing. I can tell you, right the fuck now, I don't think I've ever sprayed any tanning stuff on my body. When I got that kind of criticism, it truly made me question myself, especially as someone who grew up with Filipino culture brainwashing us all to believe white skin is better. Even in Filipino showbiz and media, I didn't see myself on TV back home, which says a lot about what is glamorized back home. I don't think people realize that even back home whiteness is glamorized, it's normalized. It's a symbol of wealth and class, strength and status. Native Filipinos weren't white. And I have to remind myself that it wasn't until Filipinos were colonized by the Spaniards that we probably ever saw somebody light.

I didn't realize beauty standards were different until I moved here. Everyone in America wants to be darker. The first time I went to LA for VidCon, some creator that I had just made friends with grabs my hand, like literally pulls it toward her, and is just like, "Your tan, who did it?"

I said, "Oh me." Which I guess made her think I tanned it

myself using products because she then followed up with, "Oh, what did you use?"

When you are a person of color and indigenous Filipino who is brown, it truly makes you spiral—comments like this and accusations of Blackfishing make me question my own fucking color. Especially because my skin tone ebbs and flows from being in the sun in Hawaii, or even just from random lighting inside. There was and are barely any darker-skinned Filipinos—either in the culture I live and work in here in America or in the Philippines—who look like me that I can pay homage to. Even the community I was born into, the Filipino community, has come after me hardcore. One time I got canceled for talking shit about the Filipino government because I didn't even live there anymore, so what the fuck did I know? People were triggered and called me selfish. (That was a questionable canceling . . . Filipino people aren't a monolith!) The other time, when I posted a video of me twerking and lip-synching to the Philippines' national anthem, "Lupang Hinirang," which violates my home country's flag law, I definitely deserved it. Let me tell you, girl, it's not fun having the entire country of the Philippines hate you for disrespecting a cultural keystone, and it's even worse when your dad finds out you caused a national outcry in your country. . . . I immediately deleted the video after the backlash, then posted, "Thank you so much for understanding, I can promise you it will never happen again, I take full responsibility and I truly am so sorry."

I've done many things that were not the best actions in the world, but every time I get called out for anything, I always apologize for it from the heart. Looking back, from what I know now, I could have done things differently when I was called out.

187

I should have avoided conflict, immediately done my research the moment I started hearing from people, and then taken accountability for my actions. You can tell a lot about a bitch by how they apologize. Periodt. I truly apologize when I know I've hurt somebody. But I also only apologize when I know that I'm genuine about the apology and that I will never do it again. When I apologize, I carry that apology with me on the internet and I carry that apology with me in real life. If I fucking tell you I'm sorry for being disrespectful, for appropriation without credit, best believe I'm never gonna do it again online and in real life, and that I know why and have taken it to heart.

I'm so glad I've been called out. It made me realize that I also shouldn't be scared to speak out about so many injustices in the world, whether about Black Lives Matter or LGBTQ issues. It's important to remove our egos and always be listening to marginalized groups—queer, Black and brown, and Filipino communities raised me, their activists and trailblazers, even when I didn't know about them, opened doors for me—and I want to be able to pay it forward, and acknowledge what they gave me.

It freaks me out that I used to be so ignorant of history, and that I used to say and do such offensive things when I was younger, because I never would now. Like I'm not even saying stuff like that in my head anymore. Having conversations with yourself and with community around race and culture, and really reckoning with the history that we haven't talked about enough—that's just part of the times that we're in now. And there are a lot of things you can do to show your allyship outside your own specific communities. I think one of them is just being a fucking decent and compassionate person. Just listening to people and taking the feedback, even when it's hard and painful, is what a decent person does. Yenno, I think callout culture is good. Sometimes it's valid to be called out. How can people who have influence over other people really ever learn anything if they get only positive feedback, if they get away with everything? If you're not called out for stupid things you've said and done, then how can you progress? We need to give each other room to grow, and to have tough conversations on- and off-line. Let's look up from our fucking phones, girl, and have more empathy for each other. I know that it's so much easier said than done, but we can at least try.

....

7 Tips for Being a Better Person Online

Andy Warhol once said everyone will be famous for fifteen minutes. If he were alive today, he might have said everyone will be canceled for fifteen minutes. It's probably inevitable to be canceled for something stupid you once did. But there are a few surefire ways to potentially avoid it.

1. Don't say offensive, stereotypical shit online. You're probably not as funny or clever as you think you are— I'm just sayin'. It's a stereotype for a reason, and if you don't know why, do some research.

2. Don't sexually harass anyone. Know people's boundaries, IRL and online.

3. Don't give your uninformed-ass opinion on topics you know nothing about. There's at least millions of other people on the internet who know more about this than you do.

4. Listen to the opinions of marginalized groups. Remove your ego for two seconds and realize that the internet isn't your stage—it's a conversation, and most of the time we just have to listen and hold space for others.

5. Don't accept things as facts and regurgitate them back without researching it yourself. See tip 3: there are millions of people who don't realize they're giving dumbass opinions on what they don't know a thing about.

6. Remember that everything is permanent. But also that we are always growing. So yes, be mindful of what you put online because it follows you for forever (you'll never be able to escape the cringe sixteen-year-old version of you if you immortalize her online) . . . *but* also try to have compassion for your past self, too, bitch. We're all learning.

7. Oh yeah, and empathy is a mood. We are *all* learning. Hold people accountable but always return to empathy.

Good luck, bitch.

FOURTEEN

The Slap(s) That Changed the World

F ame can really fuck a girl up. Which is why I'm so lucky to have a truly solid support system from my family, especially the womyn folk. My whole life, I've always been surrounded by women—I was raised by them, and I feel safe with them. I just admire everything about women. If a building was burning I'd save the women first, periodt. I'm all about energy and spirituality. Women are always more willing to have an open conversation about blending feminine and masculine energy. My gayness has always been accepted more by women. I can just be Bretman Rock, and they cherish that, they don't make me feel bad about it.

Stole this pic off my mom's Facebook

More specifically, if I were to build an army to defend myself, it would be stacked with middle-aged women and aunties. And leading the charge would be my fiercest protectors—my mom and my sister.

Let's start with Princess, because she helped start this whole thing—I owe her a lot because if she didn't interrupt me and I hadn't slapped her in the head in that early video, I would not have blown up. I've always seen my sister as my doll I could dress up and play with, and I've always seen her as my supporting actress. I'm obviously the main character. My sister's very much aware that I have main character syndrome, even though she's the baby of the family and the baby usually has the most attitude. Princess is okay with all of it—she knows that I always have to be the one sitting on the fucking throne and the center of attention. (Leo things.)

Even when we did skits together growing up, I always got to play the lead female role. Princess would always be the guy or the best friend. We'd develop the choreography together, sit all our relatives together in the backyard, and perform for them. Once we put on an Oscar-worthy remake of *Mean Girls* for our family. Not only did I play Cady Heron, I played all three mean girls. When the reviews came in, my family dubbed me the successor to Tyler Perry.

When we both tried out for KIDZ BOP and sang *Pyramids* by Filipino star Jake Zyrus, Princess would have been happy for me to make it without her. Those bitches didn't pick us anyway, but yuh, she would have thrown a parade in my honor if even only I won. By some motherfuckin' miracle, my sister was never ever jealous of me. Princess has always volunteered to be "Best Supporting Bretman." She's liked being my sidekick and second banana for our entire lives. In many ways I feel incomplete without her.

My sister and I have always been on the same page about our relationship dynamic and about fame. It's funny because once upon a time my sister was more famous than me. Princess got really good at editing Tumblr pictures, and had amassed three thousand followers, a true fan base compared to my mere five hundred at the time. I was a little bit jelly—I remember that my first thought was, I'm not the main character? I'm gonna have to fix that. And I did fix it, but damn, in hindsight I should have been more supportive of Princess at the time, too.

After I got a pretty big following making my solo videos, it still took both of us appearing together to help rocket the Bretman Rock Brand (™ pending) into the stratosphere.

When I slapped Princess in that infamous video, many people (who were not Asian, mind you) freaked the fuck out, but far more people found it totally hilarious and relatable for a brother and sister to act that way. Ever since we realized that people relate to us and love seeing our dynamic (a combo of playful and hateful), we kept making more videos. Everything is totally organic—we could not make this shit up if we tried. For example, the fact that we've never been able to just hug each other—so relatable for so many brothers and sisters (who even likes touching???), or the time the bitch brought me back a cup of ice while I was dying after we filmed a spicy ramen mukbang and I'd asked for water. I think people really like seeing us fight about regular sibling stuff the way they do with their siblings.

I admit I may call her stupid more than I should. I mean she once asked what the number to 911 was . . . I don't know how we came from the same genetic material. Another time we were having a serious moment once and she whispered to me, dead-ass, "Bret, do you think Mom's a virgin?" I don't know why she whispered it to me, as if our mom wasn't right next to us. I literally couldn't do anything but look at her for thirty minutes without answering her after she said that . . .

But there's unconditional love there, too, and I think that also comes through in our videos. My favorite thing about my sister is how resilient she is. I really admire that she's been through more life than I have. She's been a teen mom, she's gone through heart-break, mental health issues, and the whole world has been through it with her because of our videos. Girls are so mean to my sister online. It's ridiculous. Sometimes I want to turn off the comments because I think I care more than my sister does. She's heard it all. Like, "I can't believe you're so fit, Bretman, how can your sister be fat." First of all, my sister is not fat. Second, who the fuck raised you to type something like that? But my sister doesn't actually need me to protect her. She's hardheaded, and I love that about her.

My sister is beyond my best friend. My sister is BFF, blood friends forever, type of vibes—we could fight about the dumbest things one minute, slap each other across the head, but we're laughing about something the next. Is there anything more beautiful than a gay boy having a built-in, blood-related fag hag 4 lyfe? (If that phrase offends you, please pretend I said "homo honey" or "fruit fly.")

The two of us are spiritually connected. I dreamed that Princess was pregnant when she was sixteen, before she even told me. I always knew she'd be a teen mom. For whatevuh reason, the bitch let me name her firstborn Cleo, after myself. If she had been a boy, he would have been Leo. When Princess was pregnant with her son, she craved ube (purple yam) ice cream, and what did I tell you about cravings? To this day, Ezekiel likes to eat rice with shaved ice. I hope he grows out of that because, girl, you cannot be doing that shit. I know my sister won't read this book, so I can say that I really feel like part of the reason I take care of my sister's kids the way that I do is because, in a way, I'm trying to make up for how mean and selfish I was to her when we were little kids.

I can't believe my sister keeps giving birth to clones of me.

196

Also, I just love watching her kids grow. It's such a privilege to be so close to my sister while she raises her kids. I want her kids to grow up how we did, raised with so much love and Aloha, encouraged to make skits for the family and express themselves the way they wanna express themselves. In a way Cleo has grown up in front of the camera, before she could even decide whether she wanted to or not. But I don't think people realize that I've stopped making as many videos with Cleo because of how mean the internet was toward my family, people were calling her a dumb-ass, or slow. For me, as her uncle, that was a crossed boundary. Like, you are grown-ass people, who are analyzing and dissecting a child's development and how she should speak at one and a half? I felt a responsibility to teach her, and myself, boundaries. Cleo has been in so many videos she's famous in her own right at this point, and she knows it. People ask for her picture out in public. I'm all, "Why are y'all asking a toddler for a picture? She does not owe you a picture." It's not normal for a kid to have strangers take pictures of them like a zoo animal.

I'm trying to teach Cleo about consent really early. When we do any type of videos or pictures, the moment she says she doesn't want to do something, we stop. It's small things like that—learning the power of no. Because I don't know if this is the life for her yet—she's too young to decide. My sister and I love entertaining people, but what if Cleo doesn't? What if she's just a motherfucking nerd? What if she doesn't want to do mukbang videos? Before I even post anything, I show Cleo. Like, you know, even if she doesn't get it, I'm like, Cleo, can I post this? And if she just so happens to say no, I won't post.

For the longest time Princess and I were the only ones who didn't cook in our family, and we bonded over that. But now that

197

bitch is in a cooking phase because she can't be giving Cleo and Ezekiel motherfucking microwavable Dino chicken nuggets every day. I see her FaceTiming with our mom to get recipes and cooking tips, and it's the cutest thing ever. Whenever I see my sister cooking, I see so much of my mom in her. Like our mom, she can never reach anything, and her ankles crack whenever she moves. She's also tough, like our mom was with us. My mom is tough—she's had to be. It's a lot to come to a new country, work a lot, and also be an emotionally present mother, to be patient with kids when you're exhausted. But she's my mom, and she's always been clear that absolutely no one can fuck wit me when this bitch is protecting me. My mom is truly the one person that makes me feel like no one can hurt me in this world. She is my biggest shield in the world, and she's always standing by to help heal me if I need her.

My mom was right next to me when I got circumcised in third grade. I've heard in America, boys usually get it done right after they're born, and they don't even know what the fuck happened. But in Filipino culture, you get snipped later and it's a rite of passage called tuli, like your balls dropping, getting bar mitzvah'd, or your period. When I was a kid, anytime I traveled back to the Philippines, I got teased that I had an "American dick," so I finally told my mom, you need to find a bitch to cut this shit open.

It's not like there were legit doctors on every corner where I came from. If I ever needed medical attention, I only remember going to my grandma's witchy medicine man friend, called an albularyo, for treatment at his house. Once I got bit by a dog and the dude sucked the rabies out through a goat tusk then rubbed it with Filipino chilis. I don't even know how the fuk that worked but I'm alive.

My circumcision required a legit MD, though, so my mom took me to a proper hospital, then stood next to me while I had anesthetic injected into my clit. While she was numbing, my mom figured out that she'd gone to high school with the doc, and they caught up about old times while I sat on the cold hard table with my legs spread wide open. I was given three choices for my clit's new style—V-cut, head-cut, or flower petals—as if I was perusing the menu at a fancy nail salon. I'm not about to tell you which one I got (but it was V-cut).

So imagine you're on the table with your legs wide open and your dick hanging out and your mom is ranting and raving to your surgeon about how your dad cheated on her with the babysitter. Thankfully, it doesn't take long to give your vagina a haircut. The aftercare, howevuh, takes longer and is more tedious. My mom had to help me wash it with boiling hot water and guava leaves every morning for weeks before she was good as new. She's such a Filipino native woman.

Speaking of my mom, the babysitter, and my dad, you don't have to cry for my mom—she eventually got over my dad and didn't remain a virgin forever (this is for you, Princess, if you ever read this). My mom has had her fair share of boyfriends—I do have to say that she had this especially cute-ass boyfriend right after she divorced my dad. He was in the Filipino military, and he was so hot. He always carried me around shirtless, and I really think that's when I knew I was into daddies. If my mom kept dating him, bitch, I would have never touched the ground.

I think my mom does have a boyfriend right now actually. She's always so wary whenever she has a new man in her life, because she thinks we're gonna hate him. I'm like, "Bitch, if you're getting dick, I don't give a fuck. What am I gonna do, eavesdrop on your dates?" I have worse things to do. As long as he's treating you right, obviously. And as long as he's not a moocher and weird.

To be honest though, my mom didn't need anyone. It's cliché, but she is the true definition of a very independent, hardworking woman. My mom is the opposite of superficial. She doesn't give a fuck what her hair looks like, or if her outfit matches, or how big her house is. If there's a fly in her coffee, she just flicks it out, drinks her coffee, and goes about her day. (I've seen her do this more than once). She's the type to stop and smell the flowers. She actually doesn't need more than she has.

After the ugliness of what happened with my dad, my mom really instilled in me how women should be treated by men. Being surrounded by women your whole entire life, you truly realize how special women are. You learn to appreciate women and feminine energy more on a deeper level, what it means to be a mother, what it means to have a vagina and everything that comes with it. And respect. I think I respect women in a way that most men don't because of how much women have influenced the world around me.

I see makeup and I think of my grandma.

I see dresses and I think about my auntie making dresses for me.

I see food and I think not only about my mom's cooking but about what it took for her to raise three kids on her own, working her ass off for us every single day.

Almost every fiber of my being is infused with the femininity of my sister, mother, grandmothers, and aunties. (Besides my dad's long hair.) Everything that I love about myself that's feminine is because a woman I love introduced it to me, or helped me find it. I will always be thankful to my mom and my sister for nurturing and nourishing that femininity in me. They were my first muses, along with Keiffer, letting me test makeup on them or straighten their hair before work or school. I appreciate them so much for shaping who I am entirely.

No matter where I end up in life, I have this strange feeling I'm gonna end up living with my mom, because we're like sixth-grade besties. I'm gonna be one of those gays who lives with his mommy eventually—not in my twenties, thank you very much. I see her ass every day as it is. Not because she's irritating. She is. But also, Mom, when you were in your twenties, did you even think about wanting to live with your parents? That's so weird. I always tell my mom, "Let me be dumb and young for now." Let me thrive on my own. Let me learn on my own.

I'll come back to the nest when my wings are tired. I promise. Just let me take them out for a spin in the meantime.

How to Embody That Feminine Energy

- Think with your head and heart, not your ween.
- Learn how to multitask—how to care for yourself and care for others.
- Moisturize.
- Change your hairstyle when you get your heart broken (works every time).
- Work on your flexibility (and I mean emotionally and physically—maybe take some dance lessons or something).
- Drive safer! Men are 77 percent more likely to die in a car accident.
- Eat healthier (women live longer, it's a fact).
- Have more orgasms as you get older—and demand them. You deserve to have fun in the bedroom just as much as any man.

His viewing lasted about a week in our house. Every time I went near his coffin, I looked at his toes, his outfit, anywhere but his face. Thank God for my lazy eye, I can't really see well anyway—everything was blurry, and that was fine by me. I was going for the "see no evil" type of vibe.

When I finally mustered the courage to look at my dad, I cried. A lot. At first mostly because I was thinking, could they not find a better shade match for his skin? Oh God. Do they not know his son does makeup? What the fuck is this? I've devoted my life to makeup, and I could have done this better. Dad, they didn't even fill in your eyebrows, and you have the thickest eyebrows ever. Then my ADHD Leo ass was like, *When I die, could I have a viewing?* Followed immediately by, *Yeah, you're gonna have a viewing. Bitch, you really fucking think you're gonna go without being seen? Come on.*

And then I finally really looked at him—and I broke down. I saw not only so much of my face in him, but so many of my dreams. Dreams that all began here, and around this man. The dream came true. The dream my dad had always wanted for me. Fame was only a vague concept; it was unthinkable for us because we lived in the middle of nowhere. But when I look back, I remember how my dad and I used to stay up every night to watch American talent shows. How he also loved to have all eyes on him. How he'd laugh when people would make fun of me and say, "He's gonna make me rich one day." When he looked at me, he was always so confident that I would have so much more than we ever had. And he was right.

Working was ingrained in me from such an early age. My dad always said, "If you want money, you have to work." I was counting money before I could even read. I learned my colors because a twenty-peso note was orange and fifty was yellow and a thousand was blue. As I grew up, he taught me the value of money and that it was what keeps the world going. His teachings made me the businessman I am today. The constant narrative growing up was, You have to do better, you have to work toward abundance. So I think I was always destined to have money. I finally feel like I have that abundance my dad dreamed of.

My dad's casket was moved to the Catholic church for a ceremony, which overflowed with people, inside and outside. People from our town and from the next town over were there—the church was packed. Afterward the body was wheeled two miles away to the cemetery in a carriage. The family usually walks behind the carriage, but as we made our way in the unbearable heat, I looked behind me and saw swarms of my Filipino fans descending on our procession. A few asked me for selfies. I was literally getting shoved left and right during my dad's funeral march. It really fucked with me because I was crying and people were screaming, "Bretman, smile!" I was so overwhelmed and so overstimulated, I couldn't handle it anymore—I wound up getting in a car and driving the rest of the way to the cemetery.

It was so annoying and rude and inappropriate. Why the fuck would I be entertaining people at my dad's funeral? This is his day. Let me bury my dad without your cameras in my face, forcing me to smile. Let me be sad. And yet I think my dad would also have loved it, to be honest. This many people didn't even show up when the mayor who never went on *Deal or No Deal* died. We laid my dad right next to his twin in a cute little house for the two of them.

made me watch him cheat on my mom, and then he chose to leave us. That whole process was so hard for me, and I'm still living with the effects his choices had on my life. I didn't want to play any more of a role in his life—if he wanted to come, I wouldn't sponsor him; if he wanted success, good for fucking him; but I wouldn't be the one to help him. It's called boundaries, for the armchair psychologists out there. I think of Bretman Rock as two different people—the public and private versions of myself. But I actually think about my dad as two people, too. I hated him as a husband and member of the family. Yet he was a good dad to me. He was a flawed dad—but I am who I am because of how he raised me and the values that he taught me.

How can I love and hate someone so much? That is what I think about every day. I love my dad. I swear. He's still my hero. Since he died, the last year of my life has been a love letter to him. Everything I've done lately has been in tribute to my dad. He's become a new muse to me—I always find a way to tie everything I do to him. Anytime I speak about the Philippines, I bring it back to him. I'm literally growing my hair long because of how fabulous my dad looked with long hair when he was younger. He would have cried over my Nike campaign because of how much he loves sports, and he would have freaked over the *Playboy* cover because he loved to collect *Playboy* trinkets and shot glasses. (I never saw the actual magazines around, unless he hid them under his pillows.)

In 2021 I filmed an entire MTV show called *30 Days With: Bretman Rock* about surviving alone in the jungle. I had been thinking back to all the times my dad took me out into the Filipino wilderness and tried to teach me survival skills. Bitch, did you

Sometimes the best way to stay grounded
is just spending a week on the ground.

think I actually wanted to have no food, shelter, phone, or beauty products for a week, and to spend that week alone just for a show? It sucked, and I almost quit a few times, but I remembered that my dad didn't raise a quitter, so I kept at it. I wanted to impress him and make peace with him and connect spiritually with him again. I built a shelter and got coconuts from trees and learned how to build my own fire.

The last couple of years, specifically like past three years, more of my family has started passing. Like, I lost two aunties back to back. My dad, my grandparents. And I have this fear now of not being able to say what I feel, never even really getting to say bye. It's just a lesson that I'm still learning—how to be vulnerable, and how to forgive fully.

By the end of that week in the jungle, I had an epiphany about my dad. Every time I told him about things I wanted to do, he made me know that it was gonna happen. He was always the first to actually make me feel like I could accomplish anything. I will

210

never forget this man, and I've started to forgive him now. No matter how much he broke my heart, he empowered me and believed in me. And after he passed, I remembered that the only people who can truly see me as Bretman and not Bretman Rock are family. I know he'd be proud of me today.

Grief Management

Everybody grieves differently. There are five stages you'll prob go through—denial, anger, bargaining, depression, acceptance—but maybe not in any order or within any specific amount of time. I'm not a licensed psychologist, obviously, but here are a few things that helped me get through the worst time of my life, and maybe they will help you, too.

Talk about it: I've said this before, and I'll say it again. Bottling up your feelings and emotions is not healthy. Go to someone you feel comfortable with, whether a family member, friend, or a counselor, and talk it out. But also know that it's okay to just sit with the grief sometimes—just as sometimes it's okay to push it away for a little bit.

Get nostalgic: After my dad passed, I started rewatching the old movies we used to watch together—these old classic black-and-white movies we used to watch on VHS because we didn't really have much access to newer ones. I rewatched *A Streetcar Named Desire*, which just reminds me so much of my childhood (and reminded me that it was also my first gay awakening, seeing Marlon Brando for the first time). And I listened to the music he loved—he was actually such a good singer. Don't tell him I said, cuz he *will* start singing. My dad was a delusional Leo, like me. So you know, you could not tell him anything. You couldn't tell him he wasn't a rock star.

Keep up the relationship somehow: I do things to remember my dad every day, whether it's growing my hair down to my ass or listening to Blondie. I started collecting vinyl again after he passed—like a twenty-seven-disc Queen set. My dad had super long hair while I was little, and he thought that he was gonna be part of a band. He was the first one to show me Queen, and Freddie Mercury, Journey, Kiss, the Beatles, all of those long-haired guys in bands who made him grow out his hair. I also did my YouTube series where I lived alone in the jungle specifically for my dad. Somehow I always find a way to keep him close, even in the small things. It matters.

Find creative outlets: Whether it's painting, making ashtrays, designing your own tattoo in your dad's honor, it helps. And don't forget to keep up the hobbies and activities you loved before, like running or pole dancing.

Avoid escaping with alcohol: It might feel good to forget about stuff when you're partying, but that's a slippery slope. Same with acting out in other ways, like sex or drugs. The sooner you deal with reality in reality, the easier it is to move forward. Notice I didn't say move on. You don't ever forget your loved ones. You learn to live with them not being there. It takes time, but it's doable. If there's anything I've learned about being a bad bitch, it's that pain can be your friend. Don't run away, the pain only chases you longer. Let it move through you and heal from it.

SIXTEEN

Be Your Baddest Bitch Self

So why did I write a book? To be honest, I felt like it was finally the right time. When I signed with my first agency at eighteen, they asked if I wanted a book deal, and at the moment it didn't click. I was like, Girl, what is there to write about? I kept pushing it off for a really long time, because I thought my life was truly not that interesting. I didn't think I had a story anyone would give one fuk about. The only type of book I thought I had in me to contribute to the world was maybe a coffee table book of tasteful nudes, yenno, something cute. Then one day, while I was writing random thoughts in my journal, it hit me. I did have a motherfucking story to tell—I have a ton of content in my short life that I don't talk about online, that would probably

resonate with my fans, or anyone, really, like having divorced parents, being an immigrant, coming from nothing, growing up in
a house with twenty-five people, being queer, being a self-made
success story, and loving Jollibee. Who the fuck doesn't love Jollibee? If you don't, girl, I don't want to know you anyway. I know
you're almost done, but put my book down anyways.

I picked *You're That Bitch* for my title because it meant a lot of
different things to me. Obviously, it's very subjective. Like,
what is a bitch? That's open to interpretation, bitch. But ultimately, I think being "that bitch" is when you get to that point
in your life when you genuinely feel like you understand yourself. And even though it seems like every story in this book is
about me all the time (and I'm not gonna lie, it is), this is about
you, too. I thank you from the bottom of my heart for humor-
ing me while I tell stories about being a weird, gay immigrant
living the American Dream. But it wasn't my only goal to talk
on and on about myself. Bitch, the bottom line is that this book
is called *You're That Bitch*, not *I'm That Bitch*. I used "You're"
on purpose. By the end, I hope you will see yourself in at least
one of these stories, that after reading it, and my tips at the end
of each chapter, you might be inspired to forgive yourself for
the stupid things, open yourself up to healing and learning, and
realize that you don't have to be famous to have stories to tell. It
seems like everybody wants to be famous, but it's such a rare,
random thing. There are other celebrities who have had to au-
dition for years and years, studied their craft, acting, singing,
or whatever the fuk. I think I got famous because my persona is
familiar to people. I'm everybody's funny gay cousin. But even

more, I think people gravitate toward me because I remind them of the unfiltered voice that lives in everybody's head. I hope this book confirms that I'm just a real-ass bitch. I haven't always been confident—I've hated my nose, I've hated the color of my skin, my eyes go two different directions, and I have a scar under my lip from piercing it. But then I'm like, Sis, what makes me feel so good when I meet famous people is that they have acne, too. Nobody's skin actually looks that good in real life. I would still never post a picture of me with acne, but let me tell you, all these bitches have acne, girl, they got big-ass pores, they got wrinkles, and they're far from perfect. I need to go back and dedicate this book to all the bitches with acne.

And I'm not gonna lie, when I walk out the door every day, I still get scared. But that's normal. I think a little fear before you go somewhere actually shows that you know you're on the right path toward something new. You can carry your fears and anxieties, understand them, and turn it into your confidence. Every fucking time I work on anything new, at first, I always feel like I can't do it. I get impostor syndrome. Almost every time I have to pep-talk myself, tell myself that I deserve something. I know how much work I've put in, but I still always have to remind myself, "Don't doubt yourself. Wow, girl, you went through so much." There's talent in being yourself, flaws and all. And that's more empowering than even my daily morning affirmations.

It's normal to not feel like you deserve something, I think. Sometimes I think the younger me deserved the success and the comfort I have today more than I do now, because he was struggling more. When I feel this vibe, I need to remind myself that it's like someone spent twelve hours baking you cookies, and they're so excited to give them to you. And you're just like, I don't want

Bad bitches working from home
during the pandemic

the cookies. Except you are the person who baked the cookies for yourself.

I'm so lucky that I've had people rooting for me the whole way. I've had the luxury of a very open and accepting family. I've had the luxury to just be who I am. What if my mom disowned me when she figured out I was gay? I don't know what type of depression that would have sent me into. I was blessed to have the family that I have. And if they hadn't accepted me and hadn't allowed me to explore my gender and my sexuality, we would still be all in that fucking house, all twenty-five of us. That gift of acceptance at an early age is so priceless, and I feel like I owe them so much.

My fans, from past to present, we've grown up and gotten older with each other. That made me cry the other day, thinking about how so many influencers and people who get famous get

217

bombarded with comments like, "Oh, you've changed." "Money changed you." I've never gotten those comments. I think people just genuinely want me to be the best entertainer I can be. You didn't get mad at me for moving on from beauty. You didn't get mad that I stopped doing "The Science Bitch," or rating cereal, or screaming "Good motherfukin' morning BITCH" while skateboarding through my living room. You understand that some days I'm not going to post on my Stories because I'm burned out. Everything runs its course. I won't always do the same shit. That's just life. I feel like my audience has always welcomed my many and unpredictable transformations, and has loved watching me grow from a skinny young punk to the strong successful working womyn I am today. Bitch, we all have more things to accomplish.

Listen, girl, I don't feel like I've unlocked any giant secrets to life. I was a kid making choices. You don't need to put me on a pedestal or in a glass box, but I get it—I put all the people I look up to in a glass box, too. Another tweet I see all the time is "I just want to live like Bretman," or "I want to do what Bretman does." I don't think you realize you can do what I'm doing, exactly where you're at. You don't have to be from Hawaii to skate around your neighborhood with your dog, and you don't have to be where I am to also sit on your roof and make homemade ashtray molds. Whoever, wherever you are, you can be a badass bitch with lots of experiences and stories, too. Maybe you just haven't realized you can yet, or don't have the words to tell your stories right now.

I am really proud of my ability to push the boundaries of representation. I meet so many queers who tell me I inspired them to come out. Once, at a fashion show, a Hawaiian guy pulled me to the side. He was like, Bretman, you have no idea what you mean to queer Islander kids. I wish there was a Bretman Rock when I was young. I also saw a Tweet recently about me that said, "I love how Bretman is bringing back the Peacock Revolution." I looked it up, and in the 1970s, men would wear clothing that blurred the lines between women's and men's aesthetics. A lot of male artists—David Bowie, Elton John, Queen, then later Kiss and Mötley Crüe—were all wearing women's clothes. I was like, Maybe now is my peacock era. But how do I bring it forward and make it even more my own? I'm always moving the goalposts to challenge myself. I may be an influencer for millions now, but there was a time ain't nobody was watching me, and I was still out there doing my thing. I hope that inspires you to live openly and as your best, most authentic self, because you never know who you're going to affect or help. We all start somewhere.

S o you may be wondering, What is Bretman Rock is going to do next? I think the charm of Bretman Rock is that he doesn't even know exactly. I mean, I do know that I want to be known as the best entertainer of my time. Let me be clear: I don't ever want to be known for just one thing. I truly just want to always be in front of or behind the camera. One goal I've decided that I want to do is redefine the action movie genre. I don't ever want to play the stereotypical gay best friend role. Every time I meditate now, it's very clear to me that I'm gonna be a superhero in the next pinnacle of my career. Imagine hot, gender-bending gay action movies, breaking stereotypes left and right. Even just saying it right now, I feel like it's gonna happen. I think I would kill an action-comedy movie! I just need to train for it and take some acting and martial arts lessons. I mean, I have the Mortal Kombat hair going on right now, so let's not waste it.

Whatever it is, I'm ready for the next new thing. I've gotten to this point where I am letting the universe take me on a wild ride. But at the same time, I'm not going to work myself to death. I'm not going to let ambition eat me up and spit me out. Goals are always cute, and it's a good base for what you wanna do. But if I died tomorrow, I'd genuinely die happy, having come this far already. I'm truly so grateful for growing up poor; it puts everything into perspective. A friend who started a TikTok came over the other day to get some advice about making it on social media. She kept peppering me with all these questions, until I finally stopped her and said, "Bitch, like, what is your end game?"

"I just don't want to be broke."

"Sis—" I gave her side-eye. I started earning money at a young age, and it was a privilege. But I've learned that there's so more to being a content creator, and to life, than just money. If I woke up tomorrow and my bank was completely wiped out, I really would not even have anxiety about it because I'm still gonna be famous. Fame was always my drive. There was literally no word in my language for "fame" back in my village in the Philippines, but I still just wanted to be known. I just wanted people to see me. Period. Regardless if I had stayed home, I would have been a star. The money hunger that went alongside fame ended for me because there's only really so much you can buy as a fucking person, honestly. Yeah. Nobody needs four cars. It doesn't take much for me to be happy now. If you really watch my videos, it's the little things, like, Oh my God, this bitch's whole day is made just because he was able to open a coconut with a rock.

Honestly, at this point I'm more scared of just not having the passion for this work anymore. I'm more scared to wake up one day and not wanna do videos anymore, because my desire to entertain people has been what has driven me my entire life. Bitch, you best believe that if I went flat broke tomorrow, I'd start from scratch. You best believe that I'd eat a bug and contour my face again to get new fans. Most of all, you best believe I'd slap my sister right across the head and do it all over again.

Through writing this book, I fell in love with telling my whole story. I discovered that I've been one badass bitch on my journey so far—that I've been so resilient, that I can go through extreme situations and survive. I think my family is proud of me, even if they don't always say it out loud. I give them so many reasons to be proud of me, so if they forget to say it, maybe it's because it's so hard to choose. My cousins come from the same house as me and watched me soar to new heights. They don't see my success as, Oh, now we can ask him for stuff. They see it as, If Bretman did it, we can all live the American Dream. We can all dream bigger. Like, my brother and I got closer after my dad passed, and we have deep talks—he started writing poetry, and I've been reading it, and he's been telling me that it's been easier for him to wish for things, and ask for more from the world. I like to think I blessed my family with that skill, and taught them about manifesting. I've influenced my family to be better people and to attract success. I might be one of the youngest cousins, but people come to me for advice now (and I'm just like, what the fuck, sometimes I just be saying shit just to say shit, and you're still coming to me?), and we have long talks about what's next, what's possible.

The Bretman Rock you knew is the product of everything that I went through in life, but this book contains all of the stories from the Bretman Rock I know, and have gotten to know better while writing them down. It's so cliché to say, "I've gone through so much, and we've all gone through the same thing." We all have unique stories to tell. You're not gonna relate to all of my stories, but I hope you saw reflections of what you've gone through, whether it's losing your dad at a young age, immigrating to a place where you don't even speak the language, or losing your virginity at Disneyland. I might have some of the same scars and stretch marks that you have. And scars and tiger stripes are really motherfucking cute as fuck.

Thank you for going through all of this—your stories and mine—together. Now you gotta take what you learned from the book and go forth and prosper.

I'll end this whole fucking thing with the four biggest lessons I've learned so far—lessons that guide me every day.

How to Be Your Baddest Bitch Self

1. **Being nice and genuine gets you everywhere in life.** I'm a bitch, but I'm also so nice at the same time. Also I think the whole perfect facade is dying—genuineness is what we're all craving. Like on TikTok these days, we're seeing people of color who are going back to the roots of what beauty is and what it means to them. And it is so different in so many different cultures. For me, as I have gotten older, my content has been driven by intention, and that intention is to really just be as Filipino as fuck. I just wanna honor my family and always give us a good name, cuz we are kind people.

2. **Remember that nobody is perfect.** Not even celebrities! The most perfect people don't even like themselves, girl. Nobody is born knowing everything in this world, and nobody dies knowing everything either. Unless you're motherfucking Albert Einstein. But what did that bitch do? Only discovered the most obvious thing in the world, gravity. No, wait, that was Isaac Newton. Any fucking way, knowing that and

telling myself that helped me forgive my younger self. I made mistakes when I was young. I'm still making mistakes today. And I'm gonna make mistakes for the rest of my life. You don't just say sorry once, period. And bad bitches forgive themselves.

3. **Go home. Home is childhood.** Whenever I'm having a hard time, I remember the little old me. I think about him a lot. Especially when I wanna complain about what I'm doing today. I'm always like, Bitch, younger you would have killed for this. These are the dreams that your younger stuff could not have imagined. If you're ever feeling lost, go home, especially if you were raised with love and Aloha. Home is childhood, too. If you ever feel out of place, reconnect with your childhood self. We all plant seeds when we're little, and our adult selves are truly a reflection of what grows from that. Like, remember when my sister and I would perform bad skits for two cousins in our backyard? Guess what, those dumbass dynamics and theatrics manifested into our YouTube videos later.

4. **Don't take everything so seriously.** I think people forget to laugh at themselves. Also keep in mind that there's room for everybody to succeed in their own way. Think about your makeup bag, bitch. If you open it up, it's not like there's only one brand in there. I have mascara from three different brands. I have foundation from different brands that work with my skin tone. They all do the same thing, just in a different way.

There's space for everybody in my makeup bag. Like, just because I'm killing it, doesn't mean you can't too. I'm rooting for you. Life may be like a box of chocolates, but I'm lactose, so instead of shitting my pantalones, I prefer to say life is like a mansion. There's a room for everybody in there—we all just have to find our own spaces within.

Acknowledgments

There are a lot of people I would like to thank, but first, I would like to thank all of my ancestors who came before me for allowing me to live their wildest dreams. I carry each and every one of you with me in all walks of my life, thank you for guiding me and for allowing me to be celebrated.

Thank you to my entire family, especially my brother and sister, who never fail to make me laugh and annoy me every time. My beautiful mother, who showed me what a true bad bitch is. I will never be the bad bitch that you are, but I will always strive to be, you are my super woman. To my late father, who is now with me wherever I go, thank you for showing me what it's like to be a Leo. You are the reason I grew out my hair, why I balance my masculine and feminine equally, and why I look at myself and wink at every mirror I pass.

Thank you to all the mentors in my life. My schoolteachers, who were very patient with baby Bretman. My forever teacher, Dru; you didn't teach me to be funny but you taught me that I was

226

funny. You have guided me in so many ways that I couldn't even begin to list. You are the reason why I push myself to be uncomfortable, you are the reason why I work on myself to always be the bestest and baddest, and I'll forever make you proud.

I would like to thank my friends: I'm forever blessed for having the friends I have. Thank you for always encouraging me to go after it; thank you for defending me from people who didn't really understand me; thank you for seeing my light before the rest of the world did. You guys are the reason why I don't let bitches tell me shit, you guys are my power.

Lastly, thank you to everyone who made this book possible. Thank you to my writing partner, Dibs, for those hours of listening to me and my nonsense that you will never get back. Thank you to my editor, Jenny, you are such a sunshine and so patient with me. I love you! And my book agent, Albert, for pushing me to finally give the world what it needs: THIS BOOK.

Thank you, Agyamanak, Salamat, and Mahalo.

About the Author

BRETMAN ROCK is a digital entertainer, known for his unique sense of comedy and genderbending fashion, and helping to pioneer the new standard of genderless beauty. He has a combined following of over 45 million globally and may be recognized from his reality series, *MTV's Following: Bretman Rock*, or his YouTube Originals limited series, *30 Days With: Bretman Rock*. With accolades ranging from *Forbes*'s 30 Under 30 to *Variety*'s Power of Young Hollywood to Beauty Influencer of the Year at the 2019 People's Choice Awards and Breakthrough Social Star at the 2021 MTV Movie & TV Awards, Bretman continually proves that it is possible to be an international superstar and business mogul while being unapologetically yourself.